Maya

All the Best

Maya

Maya

✦

The Story of a German War Bride

Maya Torngren

iUniverse, Inc.
New York Lincoln Shanghai

Maya
The Story of a German War Bride

iUniverse books may be ordered through booksellers or by contacting:

iUniverse
2021 Pine Lake Road, Suite 100
Lincoln, NE 68512
www.iuniverse.com
1-800-Authors (1-800-288-4677)

Because of the dynamic nature of the Internet, any Web addresses or links contained in this book may have changed since publication and may no longer be valid.

The views expressed in this work are solely those of the author and do not necessarily reflect the views of the publisher, and the publisher hereby disclaims any responsibility for them.

ISBN: 978-0-595-44345-1 (pbk)
ISBN: 978-0-595-88675-3 (ebk)

Printed in the United States of America

Contents

MY ROOTS

Since I grew up in Germany under Hitler's regime, my life has been very different from people born in America.

I will start with my parents; after all, we have to thank our parents for giving us our lives. My mother, Rosa Kerber, was born June 20, 1902 in Augsburg, Germany to Katharina and Johann Kerber. She was the third oldest child of eight children (six living through adulthood, three brothers and two sisters). She told me once that she was left handed, but her father would not allow that, as at that time they thought it was evil to be left handed. So they tied her left hand to her chair at dinner time to force her to eat with her right hand. The end result was that my mother was ambidextrous all her life.

The family was poor, and when she was thirteen years old, they sent my mother into service, taking care of a household and the family's small children. It is hard for us to imagine sending a thirteen-year-old out into the world to work. My mother always told me how homesick and lonely she was. It finally was too much for her and her family took her back again.

To this day, schooling is very different in Germany than it is in the USA. A child goes to public school through the eighth grade and then on to an apprenticeship to learn a trade. If you want to go to college, you have to change schools at age nine and go to a pre-college school, which was very expensive at that time. Most people then (and even in my time) could not afford to send their kids to this school, so most only went through the eighth grade, and then on to trade school. While you are an apprentice for three years, you work regular hours for the company of your choice for less than minimum pay. You are also required to go to school three times a week to learn more about your trade. My mother chose to be in the retailing business. After her apprenticeship, she took and passed the required exam and received a certificate as a journeyman (or retailer). She lived at home with her family until her marriage to my father. Her father was very strict and still slapped her when she got home late, even when she was in her twenties, and she believed that her hearing loss was caused by too many slaps across her ears.

My father, Franz Xaver Buk, was born on January 12, 1904 in Augsburg to Maria and Franz Xaver Buk. He didn't have too great of a family life either. When he was a teenager, his mother died and his father was left with a small child, my father's sister Elsa. His father immediately got married again, to a much younger woman, and they had two more children. Because my father was left alone a lot, he had to take care of himself and found that he liked to cook. His wish was to be an apprentice to a cook. However, his father wouldn't hear of it, so he was forced to take an apprenticeship as a machinist, a choice he hated all his life. He left home as soon as he was able. This was right after World War I, and times were very bad and jobs very hard to find.

At age nineteen, he met my mother. They dated for many years and were engaged for five years. He was in and out of work and refused to get married until they could afford to get a place of their own. My mother became pregnant with me and I was born on February 26, 1929. I was told that it was the coldest day in many years. When my mother was in the hospital, the only visitors that came to see her were my father and my mother's oldest sister Mari, who was married and defied her father who forbade anybody to go and see her, including her mother. I was named after my aunt Mari.

After my mother came home from the hospital, her father ignored not only her, but also me. He acted as if I wasn't there at all. My mother went back to work again and my grandmother took care of me. Well, it didn't take long until my grandfather couldn't resist me any longer and from then on until the day he died, we were (like we say in German)"ein Herz und eine Seele" (one heart and one soul).

My mother's youngest brother Willi, who was fifteen years old when I was born, was still living at home. He told me later that he sometimes had to baby-sit me. He said he tied a rope to the handlebar of my baby buggy and pushed me back and forth, which I seemed to like a lot. He was always very protective and acted like a big brother to me.

My grandmother Katharina Kerber   My grandfather Johann Kerber

My father Franz Xaver Buk   My mother Rosa Kerber Buk

MY EARLY YEARS

In October 1931, when my father and mother got married, they let me attend the wedding reception for a short time. I was told later on that I called my mother "Schöne Mama" (beautiful Mama). My father now had a job as a beer distributor and he just loved it. Apartments were very hard to find, but a friend of theirs had a house and they were able to live there temporarily until they found something better. They finally found an apartment: two rooms, a live-in kitchen and a bedroom. The toilet was a few steps down out in the hallway. Two more families had to use it. It sure was nothing much, but it was all that was available. I was still living with my grandparents and every weekend my mother picked me up to stay with them.

My grandparents had an apartment close to the Oberhausen railroad station. Since my grandfather worked for the German Railway, they provided an apartment for him and his family. It was actually an apartment complex with apartment buildings facing four streets. They all had two stories. In the back of the buildings was a small dirt yard all around, and in the middle there was a large strip of grass. Nobody was allowed on the grass. This was strictly enforced and we children could only play in the small dirt area. We would never have dared to go into the grass area.

While I was living with my grandparents, my mother's youngest brother Willi, and my mother's younger sister, Anni, were still living at home. Anni was almost totally deaf and at that time they thought (because of her speech problem) that she was retarded. Actually, she was quite bright and took advantage of her disability all her life. People did things for her; first my grandmother, then my mother and later my sister. My grandmother was allowed to stay in the apartment with Anni until my grandmother's death. Only then did Anni have to move out and be on her own and she did alright, when she had to. My mother used to say "she is going to outlive us all," and she did outlive all her siblings and made it to a ripe old age of ninety-five.

My grandfather was a completely different man with me; he just adored me and I him. We did everything together. When the weather was nice, we would go for walks to pick wildflowers and in the winter we played cards. I had a really good time at my grandparents' house, so when it came time to go home to my parents on the weekends, I wasn't always willing. My mother told me later, that it really hurt her. Of course I didn't mean to hurt her feelings, but I really didn't know where I belonged. On April 9, 1936, my sister Gerda was born. My mother had quit her job and now was a full-time mother and housewife. Of course, that meant I had to stay at my parents apartment every day from then on. I still spent a lot of weekends with my grandparents. I also want to mention here that I was baptized Maria, but until that time everybody called me Mädie (which means "little girl" in German). Somehow girls baptized Maria were seldom called "Maria"; they were Mari, Ria, Mia and Maya. So, after my sister was born, my parents decided it was no longer appropriate to call me Mädie and from then on I was called Maya, but for my "Opapa" I would always be "Mädie".

As I said before, my father was a beer distributor; he worked for the Ustersbach brewery and delivered beer mostly to grocery stores, but also to Gasthauses (restaurants). Once in a while, Papa would let me come along on the deliveries in the truck. I liked that very much because everywhere we went I was usually given candy or chocolate. One day my father said that he had a delivery close to my Aunt Mari's house and invited me to come along. I always liked to go to my aunt's house; my cousin Helmut was almost the same age as I and we had a lot of fun together. After a delivery to a grocery store, everybody had some beer and the owner asked me if I wanted a sip. This was nothing unusual; most kids were allowed a sip of beer once in a while. Well, I didn't like beer and told them so; however, I said what I would like is some peppermint schnaps. They thought this was the funniest thing they had ever heard and, sure enough, they gave me some peppermint schnaps. After my father dropped me off at my aunt's house, she noticed that I was acting very strange. She thought there was something seriously wrong with me. When I fell off a little chair, she noticed that I was tipsy. She was so angry!! She let me sleep for a while and then we all took the streetcar back to my house. My mother was also very upset. Needless to say, from then on, I was never allowed to go with my father on his deliveries again.

We were now four people living in a two-room apartment. The sleeping arrangements were not very good. My sister's baby bed was located in my parents' bedroom. Every night when it was time for me to go to bed, I started out the night in my parents' bed. Then, when they were ready to go to bed, my father carried me from the bedroom to the kitchen, where there was a bed made up for me on the couch. I never remembered waking up during this ordeal. This situation wouldn't have been so bad had my father not been a very heavy smoker. He smoked cigarettes all evening long in the room that became my bedroom each night. We now know what that must have done to me. I was always sickly and had lots of respiratory problems. I was even sent to a clinic in the Alps twice for recuperation. No one ever mentioned that it could have been my father's smoking.

Christmas in Germany was celebrated differently from the American way. First of all, it was the Christkindle (Christ child) who brought the presents for the children. Also, the children weren't supposed to see the Christmas tree, all decorated, until Christmas Eve. Of course, this was not possible in the close quarters that we lived in. Our tree was always a short needle fir tree; it was decorated with beautiful glass ornaments in all colors and with real candles. We even sometimes had sparklers hanging from the tree. However, the candles (and the sparklers) were only lighted for a very short time and only while everybody was in the room, and were never left unattended. The only talent Papa had as a handyman was when it was time to get the Christmas tree ready for decorating. He would take some branches off the bottom of the tree and attach them where they were needed to make it look like a perfect Christmas tree. The last thing that was added to the tree was the "Lametta" (icicles). They had to hang straight down; no little strand could be astray. Our tree was always sitting on top of a table. When it was time for the Christkindle to come, Gerda and I were waiting in the other room for the final moment to come into the kitchen and there the presents were lying on top of the table, under the tree. The presents were not wrapped; they were in full sight and we could see right away what the Christkindle had brought us that year. Mama made many different kinds of Christmas cookies every year. Our favorites were the Haselnuss Makronen (hazelnut macaroons) and the least favorite were the Lebkuchen, which were hard as stone. The cookies were made at least a week before Christmas, and Mama hid them away. On Christmas Eve, we found a plate of cookies under the tree for both Gerda and me. The Lebkuchen were always left over until New Year's came around. By that time, the cookies finally were soft enough to eat, and then all of a sudden we actually liked them, (besides, they were the only ones left).

We always went to my grandparents' house first on Christmas Eve. Papa never came along. It was just Mama and us two girls. They had the luxury of a living room (that was only used on special occasions). My grandmother had an antique music box and when it played Silent Night, we knew the Christkindle had been here and that we could go into the room to get our presents. (I inherited the music box and we used the same custom for our children).

We were a very musical family. My father even belonged to a man's choir. I also liked to sing, even when I was real young. When I was about five years old, my parents would take me with them when they got together with their friends and I sang the latest Schlager (popular songs) for them, to their delight. For Christmas 1936, I received an accordion. I was in seventh heaven. They were very impressed when I sat down and played Silent Night for them. I had never played an instrument before.

One time I remember (it must have been in the third grade); we were supposed to make our own kite. We were allowed to get help from our father, but Papa wasn't very handy. So of course I asked uncle Willi to help me. When we were done, I had the most beautiful kite; it was a work of art, admired by the whole class.

My parents were still unsuccessfully searching for a bigger apartment. Then one day my mother's youngest brother Willi came to see us and told us he had found the perfect apartment for us; three bedrooms, a live-in kitchen and the toilet inside the apartment. There was no hot water, but at that time nobody I knew had running hot water, so we did not miss it. When we needed hot water, we had to heat it on the wood burning stove. The stove had a separate built in compartment (called a "Schiffle"), which always had to be filled with water. This gave us some hot water and we usually used it in the evening to fill our hot water bottle. It was made of metal, so it held the heat for a long time. In the winter, it could get very cold in the bedrooms and it was always nice to have a hot water bottle in your bed. The stove was used for cooking but wasn't too great for baking. It wasn't exactly a luxury apartment by today's standards, but for us it sounded too good to be true, and in a way it was. With the apartment came a grocery store that had to be managed and run by my mother. As I have said before, my mother was a journeyman (retailer). However, to open up your own business it isn't enough to be a journeyman; you had to pass a master exam. My mother wasn't sure she could do it, but with a lot of hard work, she tried and succeeded. She now had a "Meister Brief" (master certificate) and could start a business.

We moved to Oberhausen, a district of Augsburg (actually the one my father grew up in). The name of the street was Anton Bruckner Strasse. I want to mention that, because the Hitler regime had just changed the name of the street from Mendelssohn Strasse because Mendelssohn, the composer, was Jewish. (After the war the street was changed back to the original Mendelssohn Strasse and to make things more complicated, the street that ran parallel to Mendelssohn Strasse was renamed Anton Bruckner Strasse). Almost all of the streets in our neighborhood were named after famous composers. There were Schubert Strasse, Schuhmann Strasse and Lortzing Strasse; we also had Hans Sachs Strasse, named after a famous German poet and writer.

When my mother tried to enroll me in the local school (Kapellen Schule), the teacher said, "My class is full, I can't take any more students, but you can try the other 4th grade." As we were going out the door she said to my mother "What were her grades last year?" My mother said "She had seven A's and two B's," and the teacher said "I'll take her." All the classes except one were segregated into boys and girls classes at my school.

My new teacher's name was Fräulein U. (all female teachers at that time were unmarried). She was an enthusiastic Nazi and believed in everything she was told to teach us. One day she was talking about Aryans and said "Buk, stand up. Class, this is what a true German Aryan looks like, with blond hair and blue eyes." Everybody stared at me. I was so embarrassed and could have crawled into a hole. I didn't really like Miss U. and I don't think she liked me. She preferred girls who shook hands with her and did a curtsy when school was out. I just said "Auf Wiedersehen" and left. My sister Gerda had her later on when all the kids and their teachers were sent out of the city for their safety. Gerda didn't like her either.

We all loved the new apartment, but things changed dramatically for me. My mother didn't have much time for us any more because of the store, and so I was "stuck" with taking care of my sister. Everywhere I went, I had to take her with me. I promised myself that if I ever had children, I would not burden them with babysitting to such an extent (a promise I kept). My girlfriend Irma had a brother the same age as Gerda, so whenever we got together, my sister and her brother could play, while we were babysitting them. I remember one time when I was in school, Gerda and Siegfried (they must have been about three years old) walked away from home together. My mother was frantic; the whole neighborhood was looking for them. When I got home from school, I am ashamed to say the first thing that came into my mind was that I was glad I wasn't there and couldn't get blamed. They finally came home, hand in hand, telling us that they were visiting a pre-school and had a lot of fun there. By then my mother's worry turned into anger and afterwards the kids never did that again.

Since there was very little room in the yard behind the apartment building, we kids played out in the street. At that time, there were hardly any cars on the streets, so playing there wasn't dangerous. The boys usually played soccer and we girls had our own ball games. One of the games required us to throw the ball onto the house wall. We had to throw the ball one time straight up, which was the easiest, but then it became harder. For instance, next was two times throwing with the left hand, then three times with the right hand, then four times through one leg, five times through the other leg, six times around your back, and so on until ten times. Most of the times we didn't make it all the way to ten times because the landlord would come down and stop us from throwing the ball on his precious wall. There was also hopscotch (isn't it interesting that kids played the same game across the ocean, even though we never knew that since Germany was completely isolated from the rest of the world) and my all time favorite, playing with the Kreisel (top). You had a stick with a string attached to it, which you wrapped around the Kreisel. Then you put it down on the asphalt and pulled the string to start it spinning, and kept on hitting it with the string to keep the Kreisel going. Kids also had Schnellläufer (scooters). I just had a simple one where you had one foot on the scooter and the other on the street. Some of the kids had real fancy scooters where you had both feet on the scooter, worked a pedal up and down with both feet, and you could go real fast with them. I always wanted one of those, but they were too expensive, but sometimes the other kids let me try them out. (I see these scooters are coming back again, only they are much fancier now). Most of the kids also had fun with roller skates in the summer and ice skates in the winter. I, however, never had either since I wasn't too sure on my feet and just couldn't do it. In the winter, we went a little ways out from where we lived to go sledding. There was a big hill and we had a lot of fun there.

This reminds me that many German words are very descriptive. For instance, "Schnellläufer" means fast runner, thimble is "Fingerhut", (finger hat), suspenders are "Hosenträger" (pants holders), gloves are "Handschuhe" (hand shoes), and so on.

My grandfather sometimes came over to our house and took my little sister for a walk. So one day, after he brought her back from their walk, he was going back to his favorite bench. Then on his way home he had a heart attack in the tunnel by the train station and died instantly. It was terrible for me; I loved him so much.

After my grandfather's death, my grandmother bought a cemetery plot. These plots are passed on from generation to generation, and my sister is now the owner of it.

Cemeteries in Germany (actually all over Europe) are more like parks with lots of large trees. Each grave site is a miniature garden that is planted every spring and tended and watered during the summer and fall. Then on November first, All Saints Day, all of the graves are newly decorated with flowers and everybody goes to the cemetery that day to visit their own family graves, and also to admire all the other graves. Sadly though, usually a few days after that, the frost arrives, and kills all the flowers. Now the graves are readied for winter with evergreens and at Christmas time there might be some Christmas trees or at least a lantern with candles inside. After Christmas Mass people go to the cemetery and light the candles. It is quite a sight to see.

We didn't live too far from the cemetery and it was my job during the week to water the flowers. My girlfriend usually came with me and after we did our watering job, we explored the cemetery, (I know that sounds strange) and we also always went into the "Leichen Haus" (funeral house). We didn't have scary movies, so going to the Leichen Haus was our way of scaring ourselves. It was a huge room with glass all across in front of the caskets, and in the caskets were the people that had died during that week. However when my grandfather died, I refused to go in there, I wanted to remember him as he was when he was alive.

When I was nine years old, I had my First Communion. We celebrated it with my Tante Mari's family. Her son Helmut was also having his Communion on the same day. I had my picture taken at the same place that Mama and Papa had done so many years before. Times were good then, my mother ordered my favorite cake at the bakery next door, and it was an apple cheese cake (I am still looking for a recipe like that).

The dessert specialty of Augsburg is "Zwetschgen Datschi" (plum cake), traditionally made with yeast dough, but it can also be made with a short-cake dough. In the fall, when the plums were in season all the German housewives made their cakes at home and then took them to the bakery to have them baked in their large ovens. The people of Augsburg had a nickname; instead of "Augsburger", we were called "Datschiburger." Even today I can hardly wait for the plums to become ripe (and they are called Italian prunes here) so that I can make my Zwetschgen Datschi. I still have a "little bit of Augsburg" in me.

Since we had no refrigerator, all the food had to be purchased daily. We had three grocery stores (including my mother's), a store for milk, butter and cheese and two bakeries on our street. The butcher shop was only a couple of blocks away. When housewives were shopping with their small children, the stores always gave some little thing to the kids, like candy at the grocery store, a small bakery item at the bakery or a small cut of Wurst (sausage) at the butcher. I usually had to go shopping for milk and meat every day, since my mother was busy with the store. I remember one day I took my bicycle to the butcher shop and then walked home, completely forgetting that I rode my bicycle there. As it was getting dark my mother told me to take my bicycle down to the basement, only there was no bicycle. I finally remembered what happened and luckily the bicycle was still there in front of the store. What a relief.

I loved school; we lived very close, not even a block away. I always thought I would like to be a teacher, but I knew there was no way my parents could afford to pay for the degree that I would need. When I was nearing the end of my 4th grade, my teacher sent me and one other girl (this was an all-girl's class) to the principal. She told us, that the two of us were selected for a complete scholarship, starting at 5th grade, all the way through college. My parents were to come to the school for an interview. I was so happy, I could hardly wait to go home and tell everybody my news. The next day, both my parents talked to the principal and when I got home from school, I was waiting for the good news. However, things were very different than I expected. My parents refused the scholarship without telling me why. I learned much later that they were supposed to sign a document to give up all rights to their daughter, which of course they would have never done. I was very unhappy for a while, but kids get over things when they have to.

Gerda and I really looked forward to Saturday, when Papa took us on short outings. It was always interesting for us. He made us walk, even though the streetcars went everywhere, he said that you can see more when you are walking. There was one place in Augsburg, where there was a huge empty field (it still is there today). That is where every spring and fall, the "Plärrer" would come to town. The Plärrer is like a miniature October Fest with lots of rides, food, and one large and one small beer tent. Of course, we were always the first to go there and we had lots of fun. Some other times of the year the circus came to town, also at the same place. My father loved the circus. He usually took us early in the morning, walking around the trailers, talking to the circus people, looking at the animals. I liked that even better than going to the circus performance itself. On another of our outings, he told us that he had something special planned for us. He took us to the local jeweler and had our ears pierced. Gerda got blue forget-me-not earrings, and I pink heart earrings. My mother was shocked when we came home, but what could she do? What was done was done, and we really liked having earrings. My mother however thought Gerda was much too young to have her ears pierced (she was three years old).

On our outings, my father would buy things to bring back to my mother. Usually it was fruit, cherries, pears, strawberries, whatever was in season. We always laughed, because he told my mother that what he bought was the best. It didn't matter what it was, it was always the best. My father also liked to cook sometimes and when he made something, nobody could make it any better than him, again it was the best. We were used to his bragging and quietly laughed behind his back.

My parents' wedding picture

Opapa and Mädie

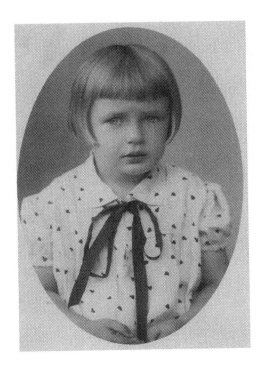

Maya four years old

Maya's communion 1938   Gerda's communion 1945

THE WAR YEARS

It was September 1, 1939 and once again the Plärrer was in town and we were having a great evening there. After going on some of the rides and strolling through all the other attractions, it was time to go to the large beer tent. There was a big Umpah band playing and everybody was singing and having a good time. All of a sudden, someone came to the microphone and announced that Poland had invaded Germany and that Hitler had declared war on Poland. Nobody clapped, nor was very happy about it. I remember that the music stopped and everybody went quietly home.

Not very long after the war started with Poland, a very good friend of my father and mother came to see us. He was a cook and was one of the first ones to be drafted into the army. He was home on leave and was telling my parents what was happening in Poland. We kids were already in bed, but I wanted to hear what was going on and left my bedroom door open. He was saying that he saw with his own eyes that the Waffen SS made the Polish civilians dig their own graves and then they shot them. I came into the kitchen where they were sitting, crying "no, that isn't true; our people wouldn't do something that horrible." My mother put her arms around me and said, "No, it isn't true." What else could she tell a ten-year-old child? I heard that man say one more thing: "I can't stand by; I have to do something!" He went back to Poland, and within a week he was "killed in action." My father never believed this; he said: "They killed him." His friend was a cook and was never even near the front lines.

I was ten years old and had just joined the JM (Young girls). All kids were required to be members of either the JM for girls or the HJ (Hitler Youth) for boys. We met twice a week and I really enjoyed myself. We played games, sang songs and had an all-around good time. Once in a great while, one of the older girls came and made speeches about how wonderful Hitler was, and also once in a while we marched to the small stadium to play ball or do running and jumping etc. I hated the whole thing about exercising and tried to get out of it any way I could. When I was twelve years old I became a Führerin (a leader) of a small group of younger girls. They all liked me a lot, because I always tried to do fun

15

things. Sometimes we went to hospitals and sang for the wounded German soldiers.

I also I remember one time we had to help a farmer to get rid of potato bugs. We had to hand pick them, and since we were all city girls, we didn't do too good of a job.

When you live in Bavaria, the customary greeting is "Grüss Gott" ("Greet God") which is still used today. Everywhere you went, this was the greeting to people on the street, the baker, the butcher, etc. But when you were dealing with government offices, the greeting was "Heil Hitler." One time I was visiting my Aunt Ria in Munich and when I entered the grocery store with her, I said "Grüss Gott," and everybody stared at me. My aunt told me afterwards that "Grüss Gott" is OK in Augsburg, but in Munich you must say "Heil Hitler" everywhere you go.

One thing that happened which affected us as a family was that my father had to give up the job that he liked so much and was forced to work in a factory. He was never in the army as he was deferred for health reasons. From then on, my father wasn't any fun anymore. He was always in a bad mood when he came home from work, and we all tried to stay out of his way.

When I was growing up in Catholic Bavaria, we not only celebrated birthdays, but also "Namenstag" (Name Day). Almost everybody had a name that could be found in any calendar, where all the Saints were listed by name. Since my name was Maria, my name day was September twelfth. We never received any big presents, either for birthdays or name days. These presents were usually just something small. It was the thought that counted. On my name day in 1940, my mother gave me a friendship album. Most of my relatives, and many of my school friends, wrote little poems or sayings in that book. There were rules set by me about how the writing should be displayed, and I used to be upset when they weren't followed. One of the rules was that on the right hand page, there should be writing and on the left hand there had to be a hand-painted or drawn picture. No paste-up pictures were allowed. That way I ended up with very nice pictures in my album. I was especially proud of one picture. It was done by the uncle of one of my class mates. He was a professional artist. It is a picture of hollies, very beautifully done. Some of the poems were interesting too. My Cousin Helmut wrote this:

Willst du glücklich sein im Leben	If you want to be happy in life
Trage bei zu andrer Glück	Be sure to make others happy too

ket made out of copper wire that they probably found in the trash. There was a note with it that said to give it to your children as our thanks. I have never seen my father cry before or after, but he had tears in his eyes, and of course so had we.

There was one more incident at his job site. The factory also had DPs (displaced persons) working for them. One was a really old man; I think he was a Russian. He was very weak probably for lack of food. One day, a foreman started to hit the man because he wasn't working fast enough. I must say here, that my father never hit anybody in his life before, but he started to beat up that foreman. The same day, my mother got a visit from a mutual friend who was also a foreman in the factory where my father worked. He was to tell my mother that "if anything happened like that again, Franz would be sent away to the concentration camp and you know what that would mean to you (my mother) and your children." The man was a nice guy; he said he didn't like it either what was going on, but as you can see, there wasn't anything we could do about it.

After the war was over and Augsburg was occupied by American troops, the owner of the very factory where these incidents occurred wined and dined the highest officers of the occupation troops. I guess there is no justice in this world. Also, while we had nothing but potatoes to eat and were close to starving, we heard later, that Klaus Barbie, the Nazi "Butcher of Lyons" lived in luxury in a villa outside of Augsburg, because he had some information about the Russians that the Allies were interested in. He later moved to South America with American help. After nine years, justice finally caught up with him when he was extradited to France, where he was convicted and spent the rest of his life in prison (a sentence too lenient in my opinion).

When I was in 8th grade something happened in our class. All the teachers we had, taught us everything that was in the textbooks, but Miss Steinle, our seventh and eighth grade teacher did sometimes show her own opinion about the Nazi regime. She never came really out with it, but you could tell that she didn't agree with everything that was written there. In our class was a girl, actually the most beautiful girl in the class. She was only fourteen years old and had a relationship with an older man. She was supposed to be taken out of school, but the girl thought if she could incriminate our teacher that would help her. Well, she told someone that Miss Steinle was speaking out against the government to us. When we came to class the next day we were taken one by one to be interviewed by the Gestapo to see if it was true that Miss Steinle was a traitor. After the interview each student was sent home, so there was no way to tell anybody what was happening. Well, the whole class, one by one told them that this was not true, we all stood by our teacher. The next day, all she said "Let's get to work, we have lost enough time", but we could see that she had tears in her eyes (I saw her many years later, after the war; she became the superintendent of schools in Augsburg.)

Although the school I attended was a public school, everybody there was Catholic. Once a week a Kaplan (chaplain) came to our school and gave us lessons in religion. I know that is hard to understand that there was religion in school in such a regime. We also prayed every morning, just like American kids say the pledge of allegiance, we prayed for the Führer. It went something like that:

Gott segne unser Vaterland	God bless our fatherland and
den Führer den Du uns gesandt	the leader that you sent us.
Gib Kraft zu seinem Werke	Give energy to his works, and
von unserem Volke nimm die Not	from our Nation take away the misery
Gib Freiheit uns und täglich Brot	Give us freedom and daily bread
und Einigkeit und Stärke	and unity and strength

This is prayer in school, Nazi style.

My parents were not regular church goers, but my mother insisted that Gerda and I attend church every Sunday. She told us: "Once you are grown up, you can make up your own mind about religion." We lived very close to St. Peter and Paul church and we heard that the housekeeper (who took care of Father Kerker and the chaplains,) complained a lot about the Father, because he often gave away their food before she had a chance to cook it. This was during the war, when we all had to depend on our food rations.

My girlfriend and I usually went to the eleven o clock service Sunday morning. I remember it was so cold in the winter, because the church was not heated.

When I was fourteen years old I was supposed to join the BDM or Bund Deutscher Mädchen, (group of German girls). The meetings were in the evening and one time some older girls took me along. When I got home that night, my parents said that this was the last time I would be able to attend, since they thought that a fourteen year old girl should not be out at night without her parents. That was the end of my BDM "career".

Once a week we had handarbeit (needlework) for a couple of hours. Two teachers tried to teach us how to knit, embroider, sew, etc. It wasn't one of my favorite classes. Strangely enough I liked math and history better. One day the girl who sat next to me told the teachers that her money was missing. The teachers came to me and said it must have been me that took that money. I was so shocked that anybody would think that I was stealing from a fellow student. I just got up and left the room and school and went home to my mother and told her all about it. Nobody was ever allowed to leave the school during school hours, but I just didn't care. I was innocent and I was just not going to take it. My mother closed the store and went back with me to school to tell the teachers what she thought of them. Lo and behold while I was gone, the money appeared again and the teachers apologized to me and my mother, but I could never forgive them. To this day I always feel strong sympathy for someone who is unjustly accused of something he or she didn't do.

Next to our school yard, the school had a very large vegetable garden. Sometimes we could work in the garden, which always was a lot of fun for us. We also learned how to cook and used the vegetables from the garden in the class. All this was happening in the 8th grade. To this day I enjoy gardening and I have always had a garden since moving to the U.S.A. We always lived in apartments in Augsburg and we never had room for gardening.

After I graduated from 8th grade at age fourteen I got an apprentice position with a mail order firm (like Sears or Wards). I had to work full-time, but still had to go to school three times a week where we learned typing, shorthand, bookkeeping and everything else that you need in business. We used to say "wouldn't it be great if they would bomb our school." Well, you should always be careful what you wish for, because our business school was completely destroyed Feb. 25/26, 1944.

We had three departments where I worked, purchasing, sales and distribution. As apprentices we were supposed to learn all aspects of those departments. I started out in sales, which meant opening letters, sorting them etc. I had a boss from Berlin. Now at this time, Bavarian people didn't care too much about people from the north. However, she always treated me well (unlike the boss from purchasing). Everybody really liked the boss from the Lager (warehouse).

Since we were now almost five years into the war, we didn't keep any merchandise in town. Most of the warehouses were outside of town, and some times the wares had to be unloaded at the nearby train stations. I wanted so badly to go along to unload some merchandise. Finally one day, the warehouse boss came up to me and said "Do you want to go with us to load up the merchandise on the truck?" I said "I sure would like to, but I don't know if my boss will let me go". He said "don't worry about it; I'll get it straightened out with her when we get back". So off we went in a truck, the driver and the boss up front, me and three other girls, all older than me on the truck bed. As we were driving out the driveway I saw my boss waving at us and yelling "Buk, come back here", but we didn't stop, and on we went …

As we were driving out in the country, all of a sudden there was a low flying airplane above us. Some of the girls said, "I have heard that sometimes the Americans throw down candy to girls". Well, this time it sure wasn't candy that came down at us, they started shooting at the truck. The driver stopped the truck and we all jumped into the ditch. The plane came back several times shooting, but luckily didn't hit us. The truck was empty; there was nothing to shoot at. After that experience we arrived at our destination, a very small train station out in the boondocks. There was only one railroad car sitting there. This is where our merchandise was and we had to unload it. We barely got out of the truck when American fighter planes started to shoot at our railroad car. We all crawled under the railroad car. It was very safe, because it was filled with mostly clothing. After that, our boss said that we would give up for the day. Since we were so close to his home, he told the driver to drop him off at his house so he could see his family and have lunch there. Then we went up to the nearby Bismarck's tower, a local landmark up on a hill where we ate our lunch. All of a sudden a group of bombers flew over us and there was one very loud explosion. The bombers must have just come back from a raid and had a bomb left that was dropped on the little village below us. We had enough excitement for a day, but the worst was yet to come. When the driver went down to pick up our boss, he found that it was the house of our boss that was hit, and he, his wife and three-year-old daughter, all were killed. When we came back to our firm, everybody was so shocked. We all cried, and the only thing my boss could say to me was "I am glad you are safe".

It was February 25, 1944; it seemed like a typical day in the last years of the war. I was fourteen years old today and would celebrate my fifteenth birthday tomorrow. In the afternoon the siren blew. I was already home from school, my father was at work and my mother, my seven year old sister and I went to the basement as so many times before. We had been lucky so far and were again, as we found out, after the all clear siren, that only Messerschmitt and some other big factory were bombed by American planes. We thought that it was a good idea to bomb the factories for then the war would be over sooner. However 260 workers and sixty people who lived close to Messerschmitt died during that raid. We didn't hear too much about that because much worse was yet to come.

We all went to bed and were awakened about 10 PM by the howling siren again. We barely made it down to the basement this time. We already heard the tremendous roaring sound of airplanes over our city; these were the English bombers that always bombed at night. (The Americans only bombed in the daytime). We weren't really frightened at that time, because we thought, "they were just flying over" as they did so often. All of a sudden all hell broke loose. I lived in a five-story apartment house at the time and it felt like the house was falling down. So now we knew that this time it was meant for the town of Augsburg. The first attack lasted two hours, (fire bombing to light up the city) and now it was 12 o'clock AM and it was my birthday. In 1944 things were pretty bad; we didn't have much food, hardly any luxuries at all. Somehow my mother had saved a bar of milk chocolate for me, my one and only birthday present.

There seemed to be a lull at that time and the men went upstairs to see what was happening. By the men I mean my father who was deferred from military service because of health reasons and two or three other older men from our apartment building, the rest were women and children. They could see that much of the town was burning, some places real close by, and they also could see that our church St. Peter and Paul was burning. While this was all going on, Hansel, a fourteen year old boy from our building, had the brilliant idea that we could see things a lot better if we would go up to the attic. So the two of us raced up to the fifth floor to look out the window. We barely made it up there when a new attack started. We came running down the stairs. Our parents were frantic because they didn't know where we had gone to. Now the second phase of destruction was starting, this time with explosives. It lasted from 1 to 3 AM. My beautiful hometown of Augsburg was in ruins, a town that was almost 2,000 years old.

We heard later on that after five phosphor bombs hit the church of St. Peter and Paul (which was built in the year of 1206) Father Kerker was on watch in the church all by himself when he saw fire coming through the ceiling. He said in his own words "I wanted to climb up to the upper parts of the roof with a fire extinguisher, but the smoke was so dense that I could not get through. We only managed to save the sanctuary and some priceless artifacts that we could carry in our hands." That night Augsburg lost ten more churches. The fire department never came; they were just too busy everywhere else. It also was a very cold night and many of the firemen's hoses were frozen.

During that night, there were 4368 fires, 730 people died, 1355 were wounded, 90 000 people were left homeless and 2790 buildings were destroyed or heavily damaged, many of them hundreds of years old. 594 aircraft took part in this raid. Sadly, the center of town, where mostly civilians were living, was the target of this raid.

The following poem was written by a fellow Augsburger and published in the local Augsburger newspaper.

GANG DURCH DIE VATERSTADT	WALK THROUGH THE FATHER TOWN

Ich gehe wieder durch die Strassen
der lieben alten Vaterstadt
darin ein Zauber ohne Massen
mich immer tief beseligt hat.

I walk again through all the streets
of my dear old Father Town
its magic without bounds
always enchanted me.

Nun aber hat des Krieges Schrecken
auch diese alte Stadt bedacht,
und jetzt ist wenig zu entdecken
von ihrer schönen alten Pracht.

But now the war's great horror
has come to the town I call home,
gone is the beautiful splendor
of all that I have known.

Kunstvolle Giebel sind geborsten,
das stolze Rathaus brannte aus,
Der Efeu rankt sich um das Haus,
am alten Tor die Krähen horsten.

Artistic gables are destroyed,
The proud city hall is but a shell
Ivy now winds around the house
at the old gate where only crows are doing well.

Es starb die liebe alte Stadt,
und nichts hat sie zurückgelassen
als Trümmerberge,
morsch und matt.

The dear old town has died,
and nothing has it left us
but mountains of ruins
decaying and lifeless, far and wide.

Ich gehe wie vom Krieg erschlagen
durch alle Winkel, tot und stumm,
gequält von einem wehen Fragen
Liebe Vaterstadt—warum?

I walk destroyed by war,
around all the corners, dead they lie
tormented by an aching question
Dear Father Town—"WHY"

Sixty years later, as I was writing my life story, I showed the pictures of my destroyed home town of Augsburg to my nine year old grandson and he said only one word to me, "why?" I didn't have an answer for him.

That day the sun never came up. The whole town was covered with smoke.

We were lucky; the apartment house was still standing, but all the windows were blown out, there was no power and it was the coldest night of the winter several degrees below zero. The fire fighters had a hard time, because the hoses froze. There was no way we could stay in our home, so we packed just the bare necessities into a little wagon and set off first to my grandmother's house, to check if she was alright. Her apartment had more damage than ours, so we persuaded her to go with us to some of her relatives about twenty miles west of Augsburg.

When I was growing up, women and girls only wore dresses and skirts, never any slacks. Since it was so bitter cold, Mama told me to put on one of my fathers long pants, which I did. I stuffed them into my boots and tied a rope around my waist, so they wouldn't fall down. (My mother never wore any slacks as long as she lived, I however got used to wearing them around the house all the time. I remember one time I was wearing a skirt and my youngest son said "Mom, why are you wearing a curtain?" He was very small at the time and I had to explain to him that I wasn't wearing a curtain, but a skirt).

It was morning by now, but you couldn't tell, since the sun was obscured by all the smoke and debris. I don't remember how long it took us to get to Batzenhofen; I am sure many hours by foot. There were six of us, my mother, my father, my sister Gerda, my grandmother and my Aunt Anni. When we got to our relatives they welcomed us with open arms, but they didn't have room for all of us. So I stayed with the local people that managed the post office. Batzenhofen at that time was a little village and the post office was in their home. They had children our age and I felt quite good about being there. I must mention here how kind those people had been to us. We were complete strangers, but they treated us like family. About a week after that huge air raid, my father went back to Augsburg to our home. He also had to go back to work. He managed to make the apartment livable again and after a few weeks we followed him back home again. I liked living in the country so much, I didn't want to go back to the city, but I also had to go back to work again.

Soon after the devastating air-raid, the city of Augsburg started with the cleanup. First of all they searched for architectural parts that could be used again, such as the tops of the Rathaus (City Hall) and Perlach tower. They found them several streets away, but still in good condition. (Today Augsburg shows itself again in all its beauty). They had little trolley trains going through town to collect all the rubble. They looked something like the ones they use in mines. All the rubble ended up at one site in town and this was later turned into a large sports stadium. Everybody helped; I remember cleaning cement off bricks, myself.

We had two POWs (prisoners of war) working for us, one was an American and one a Russian, his name was Alex. When there was an alarm, we had to carry our typewriters down to the basement with us. We were always so impressed when the American helped us carry them. Alex however was always the first one down the basement. The two men were dropped off every morning, and picked up after work. They had it pretty good there. As a matter of fact, we were jealous when the American ate all the goodies that he was sent from America in his Red Cross package. Chocolate, what's that, we hadn't seen chocolate for a long time.

Around this time, my mother gave up the grocery store. She had severe headaches (migraine) every day and just couldn't manage the store any more. Luckily the apartment above us became available and so we moved upstairs. Now that they had lost the income from the store, they decided to rent out one of the bedrooms. Our first renter was an old bachelor. When he didn't come home one day, my parents got worried and went to the police. We then found out, he had been killed in one of the air-raids. Since he had no relatives, nobody claimed him. It was quite a shock to us.

From now on things were never the same again. Augsburg, a beautiful old town, almost 2000 years old, was in ruin. It took a long time to get back to a somewhat normal life again. All the primary schools were closed and the children were evacuated to the country. The farmers were required to take in the children from the city. Some kids hit it very good, others very bad. My little sister didn't have it very good. She was a city girl, seven years old. She had to help herding the cows. She had never been that close to a cow before and now she was supposed to watch them in the meadow. The farmer wasn't too bad, but the farmer's wife made her feel unwelcome. Gerda was so unhappy, she cried every time we visited her but there was nothing that we could do, we weren't allowed to bring her home, since there were no elementary schools left in Augsburg.

Gerda had her First Communion in Oberrammingen, the little village where she had been staying since the big air raid on Augsburg. For her there was no new dress, (she was wearing the dress I wore on my Communion) and no white shoes. Even the candle was short, because it had been used before by me. There was no cake, no celebration after church, and no photographer to take her picture. We only have a little snapshot of her, in front of a barn, in my communion dress. She describes herself now as the poor little "Baura Mädle" (farmer girl) in the photograph.

After the war and as an adult, Gerda would never set foot into this village again that was so filled with bad memories for her. Many years later her husband Sepp one day drove there with her and told her that she had to face it, to finally get over her bad experience as a child.

At that time I was having problems with my hands, for some reason I got warts all over them. I went to the doctor and he removed them, but told me to be very careful and not to get my hands in any soapy water. A friend of mine, who also had a sister in the same place as my sister was, found a ride for us to visit them. When I got there the farmer's wife said, "If you want anything to eat, you have to work for it." What she wanted me to do was wash the laundry. I told her that I couldn't get my hands in soapy water, but she laughed and gave me a brush and said, "Just do it." I never had to wash any clothes before; my mother always did that for me. I did what the woman told me to do, and was I ever sorry afterwards. The next day both of my hands were badly infected. My doctor said "what have you done to yourself?" When I told him, he got real mad and said "Those damn farmers." This wasn't the only experience I had with "damn farmers". Food was very scarce for us city dwellers. So one time when we were on our way home from visiting Gerda, we stopped at a farm and were told that we were going to get some "Fleisch Küchle" (meat patties). We hadn't had any meat for a long time, so that was great for us. I thought when I started to eat them that they smelled a little funny, but we were hungry and we ate the whole lot. When I came home I was so sick to my stomach. I am sure I had food poisoning.

By the start of 1945, things really got out of control. We had one air raid after another. Sometimes I started out in the morning to go to work and while I was riding the streetcar, the alarm siren would go off. That meant everybody was supposed to find shelter any place they could. My mother was so worried about me, because she never knew where I might be at a given time. We didn't have a telephone, so I couldn't tell her that I arrived safely at my place of work. The raids continued and by the spring of 1945, we couldn't get any work done at all anymore. We spent most of our time in the bunker, or on our way to or way back from the bunker. There was a real safe bunker not too far from my workplace and we decided to go there, rather than just the basement where I worked. After some major damage to the offices, the company decided to close down its business altogether.

Then I worked for a little while at the nearby shoe factory. My girlfriend Anni already worked there, and I knew it was only temporary. When we parted after work, we would say to each other "See you tomorrow, if we are still alive," not a great greeting for a couple of teenagers. The best part about working at the shoe factory was that I could get more to eat using less food coupons at their cafeteria every working day than I could at home. That left more food for the rest of the family.

By the end of the war, we had altogether nineteen air raids on Augsburg with 1500 people dead (civilian casualties). We knew what war was like and by now, most of the new generation of Germans is very reluctant to enter any wars. This is something Americans should consider when they complain about Germany not wanting to go to war in Iraq. (Although Germany did send over 2500 troops to Afghanistan to help the U.S.A. after 9/11, and several were killed. The Germans are still helping us there).

I have heard some people here in America talk about World War II as the "good war." Well, from my own experience I know there is no such thing as a good war. The people that suffer the most are the civilians, which is of course the case everywhere, especially now in Iraq. One thing that has improved since my time in the war: at least now the civilians aren't the target anymore, as was the case in World War II on all sides. However there are still a lot of civilian casualties in the Iraq war and I feel so sorry for the innocent people over there. I always think it is cruel for President Bush to say "We are fighting the terrorists over there (in Iraq), so we don't have to fight them over here," as if the lives of the people over there were less important than American lives.

In the beginning of 1945, the German military in Augsburg told all the remaining old men and young boys over sixteen to report for training to defend their homeland. My father and my Cousin Helmut who was sixteen years old were in the same group. They called them the "Volkssturm" (the People's army). They were given American army coats (it was very cold at that time) since there were no German uniforms available. They were never given any weapons. The one time they got together, they were supposed to learn how to march. Well, one group went this way and the other that way. They were completely out of control. The officers finally gave up and told them to go home. They all kept their American overcoats. Years later my father and my Cousin laughed about the day they were in the "Volkssturm." Unfortunately the young boys up north didn't have it that good. Many very young boys were killed in the last days of the war.

In April 1945, we were told that the Americans were just outside of Augsburg and if we didn't capitulate, the entire town of Augsburg would be leveled. My mother said "We are not going to wait for that, we are going back to Batzen-hofen," which we did. Again with our little wagon we took off, once again stopping at my grandmother's house to pick her up. However, this time she refused to go with us, saying she was tired of running away. She said "I will just hang out my white sheet and hope and pray for the best." So it was just my mother, father and I who made the long walk again. My father wasn't very thrilled about going either, but my mother was determined that she was not going to stay in town. After we arrived, I stayed with my friends at the post office again. They were such nice and kind people. Shortly after our arrival, all of the men of the village had a meeting to decide what they could do to help with the war effort. My father was invited too. Some of them decided that they should blow up the little bridge over the Schmutter creek, but my father told them "The Americans came across the Rhein River, do you think a little creek is going to stop them? It will just make them mad." Well then, they all agreed and decided to wait and see. We heard that the Americans were very close to us and to be safe, we all waited in the basement. Sure enough very soon after, some GI s came in with their weapons drawn, scaring us half to death. Nobody knew any English, so we didn't know what they were saying, but we figured out that they were just looking for German soldiers or weapons. We had neither and they left again.

My mother wouldn't let me out of her sight after the Americans came. I was sixteen years old, and she was afraid that the soldiers would hurt me, which of course didn't happen at all. After a few days, we heard that Augsburg had surrendered without anybody getting hurt. I found out much later about the details of that surrender. We all went back to Augsburg again. Thank God, the war was over for us.

This is the story of the Surrender of Augsburg according to the "Augsburger Allgemeine" newspaper dated April 28, 1995:

During the night from April 27 to April 28, 1945, the city of Augsburg had to decide if it would surrender peacefully to the 7th U.S. Army located just outside of town, or if it would be defended by the remaining German troops. A very brave and realistic group of men decided that there was no way they would allow their beloved Augsburg to be completely destroyed. They called themselves "the Freedom Movement." One of the men was the Lord Mayor of Augsburg who had been in that position since 1934, but he had been also a member of the Nazi Party. At 9 PM the Mayor organized a meeting with the prominent Nazi government officials and the German Military Town Commandant General Fehn. The freedom group suggested that the city should surrender. "I will never capitulate," said the General and the meeting broke up at 10 PM with nothing resolved. The Mayor suggested that everybody should go to the Bunker at the Riedinger Haus. The General agreed and everybody arrived there at 11 PM. In the meantime, the

Mayor tried to get in contact with the American Army, but the German troops had cut all the telephone lines. The Mayor asked Dr. Lang to try once more to get in touch with the Americans and in the early morning hours he finally did get through, and he was told by the Americans,"This is your last chance to surrender your town or else Augsburg will be reduced to ruins and ashes." At that time General Fehn tried to take the phone away from the Mayor, but the Mayor just hung up. When the General left the room the Mayor called the Americans again. He identified himself as Lord Mayor of Augsburg and told them he was in charge and he was willing to surrender. The Americans said, "We will be with you soon." It was decided that some men on the outskirts of Augsburg would lead the Americans into the city, but they couldn't reach the Mayor anymore as all the lines had been cut once more. Soon the whole group was in the Riedinger bunker. Twenty-seven men of the Freedom group led the Americans to the bunker and they all went inside. It was now 6:20 AM. General Fehn, his aids and all the Nazi officials were completely surprised. The German General asked for permission to make a phone call to his troops. However, the freedom group didn't trust him and would not let him make the call. Then the American Commander O'Connell told everybody "The time is up" and immediately arrested everybody. Just then one of the Nazi officials shot himself in another room. At this time, two jeeps arrived with the young man who had led more Americans into town. I will tell his story next. By 8:00 AM, the whole town of Augsburg was in American hands.

The young man who led the Americans into town was Hubert Rauch, a twenty year old soldier stationed at the military debarkation station just outside of Augsburg. The Reserve Major who was in charge of this group was Dr. Klaus Mueller. On April 23, 1945 the young soldier had confessed to the Major that he was a member of the freedom group. The Major told him of the big risk he was taking and immediately discharged him from the army. Rauch had been a member of the group since 1944. His time of action came on April 27, 1945. All telephone contacts were broken and by midnight it was decided that they needed more people to lead the Americans into the city from the other side. Rauch volunteered and left on a bicycle with a very important message in English, "Follow the bearer of this letter. He will lead you through the town of Augsburg to the place where you can arrest General Fehn." He tied the message around his waist and left. He didn't get very far when an American soldier arrested him. It was now around 3:00 AM. He tried to tell the soldier that he had a very important message for the Americans, but the soldier didn't listen and Rauch was locked up in a room with some other German civilians. After the changing of the guard, he finally convinced another soldier to look at his important message and he brought him to a German speaking officer. That officer realized the importance of the message and took Rauch to the commanding officer who told him that they would take two jeeps with white flags and that's how they would drive through town. Rauch tried to persuade him not to fly the white flags, since he wasn't quite sure if all the bridges had been secured by the freedom group. However, the American commanding officer insisted that the flags stay and that he, Rauch, would be in the first jeep and he in the second. Everything went without a hitch and they arrived just in time to see the first American group leading General Fehn and his group out of the bunker. They all got out of the jeep and the Americans saluted the German General as he was led away. Since Dr. Klaus Mueller never was a member of the Nazi party, he was installed as the first Lord Mayor of Augsburg after the war.

Maya as a "Jungmädel"

Uncle Willi, an officer in the German Army

THE IMMEDIATE POST-WAR YEARS

The very first thing we wanted to do after the war was to bring Gerda, my little sister, back home. We weren't able to do that right away because there was no transportation available. Nobody had cars, and it took a while for public transportation to work again. But soon Gerda was home again with her family.

During the first few weeks of the occupation we had a curfew. Nobody was allowed on the street after 8 PM. After the evacuation of the school kids and their teachers, the Kapellen Schule was used to house French POWs. They were free now and could hardly wait for their transportation back home. Across the street from the school, the Americans took over a four-story apartment house. The people who lived there had to get out in two hours and leave most of their things behind. After curfew, the only people on the street were the American and French soldiers. We were watching from the window (an old German custom) to see what was going on. We thought it quite funny to see the American soldiers throwing a ball back and forth and each had what looked like a huge leather glove on one of their hands. While they were doing that we saw that they were constantly chewing something, what we didn't know. The Frenchmen were just as intrigued as we were. I thought they would be buddy buddy with the Americans, since both of them were on the winning side, but they hardly socialized with each other.

My tobacco-addicted father noticed that the Americans often threw away barely smoked cigarettes. He told us girls to pick up the butts and bring them to him. Gerda didn't mind, but there was no way I would stoop so low as to pick up cigarette butts. He also had another job for us to do. One of his co-workers had a garden and he was growing tobacco. Germany certainly does not have the climate to grow tobacco, but evidently he grew some big leaves that he dried and used himself. My father got the stems that were left after stripping off the leaves. He came home with a big bag full of stems and my mother, my sister and I had to cut them all into little pieces. He then rolled them in a piece of newspaper (no other

35

paper was available) and smoked it. Addiction to cigarettes is a terrible thing; my father died of lung cancer at the age of sixty-two.

Shortly after the war, I was still working at the shoe factory with Anni. We liked to sing together, and we really sounded good. Once we even thought of participating in a talent show, then in the last moment we lost our nerve. One time a young man who worked at the factory told us he heard that we liked to sing. He belonged to a youth group and said that they really would like for us to join them. This sounded real good to us and we went to our first meeting. We had a lot of fun and were thinking of joining. The next meeting we were told that they would have a "guest speaker." We were shocked to find out that this group was a communist youth group. Of course, they never saw us again after that. Was I ever glad that we found that out in time!

When the war was over and things got back to almost normal again, my father's half sister Rosa who was nineteen years old (I was sixteen at the time) and her girlfriends were dating American soldiers. One day she came to my house and asked if I could come over to her house with my accordion. She wanted me to play for her friends, so they could dance. I did go over to her apartment and played some of the German songs that I knew how to play. However the soldiers wanted to hear American songs. I told them I didn't know any American songs and asked them to sing some to me. So this was the very first time I heard an American song. It was "You are my sunshine, my only sunshine." I usually could play a song after I heard the melody only once. Those soldiers were so happy and urged me on to play more songs. We all had a good time together. That also was my first contact with Americans. I didn't know any English then and I decided it was essential for me to learn English. I took several classes; English was very easy for me to learn.

1946 and 1947 were probably the worst years for us food-wise. If we didn't have potatoes, we probably would have starved. For instance, we were allowed 100 grams (less than a quarter pound) of meat and fat per person per month, hardly any flour, very few vegetables, and very little bread. I remember going "window shopping" with my mother and sister for bread at the bakery. We found out later that my mother very often went without food so we had something to eat and she was an expert when it came to cooking with potatoes. Nothing really tasted good, since we didn't have any salt or onions either. I remember one time we were told we would get a care package from America. When we opened the bag, there was nothing but beans in it. We had never seen beans like that before and didn't know what to do with them. It sure would have been nice to have been told how to cook them. I know we never ate them. This is the only thing we ever received.

The whole economy was based on cigarettes. You could get anything for cigarettes. So of course that left us out completely, since we didn't have any. As I said before, 100 grams of meat isn't very much but if you bought your meat at a horsemeat butcher you received three times the amount. There were hundreds of people standing in line and my mother, my sister and I had to take turns. The lines would be four to five people deep and go all around the block. When it was my turn to stand in line, I always made sure I was in the center of the line so that nobody I knew would see me. After all, a seventeen year old girl had some pride. People always say if you are hungry enough you will eat anything. Well I guess there are some exceptions to that rule, mine was horsemeat, I would not eat it, and my mother's was ..., we'll come to that! One day my father came home with a big package of meat. My mother wanted to know what it was, but my father said, "Just cook it and after we eat I will tell you what it was." Well, my mother cooked it and made a great Sauerbraten out of it (we still had some vinegar left) and my father, my sister and I ate it and liked it very much. My mother would not touch it. After we were done eating he told us that we had just eaten dog meat (a Saint Bernard). Somebody at work had given it to him, and he didn't know where it came from originally. My mother would not eat any of it, but we kids thought it actually was very good. Later Gerda embarrassed my mother by calling up from the yard "Mama, is there some more of the dog left to eat?"

By the winter of 1946/47, we ran out of coal. We always had the coal delivered, several Zentners (100 pounds) at a time. They would use a coal chute and pour it directly into our cellar. We didn't have central heating; all we had was a Herd (stove) that could be heated either with wood or coal, or both. This stove was used for cooking and heating the kitchen. We now had no heating material left. Sometimes my father came home with his briefcase full of wood if he was lucky enough to find some scrap wood, which was barely enough to heat the stove for cooking. One day, Gerda's girlfriend's mother came to my mother and told her that out by the Gaswerks was a big pile of coal. So my mother, Gerda, Irene and her mother took the little wagon, two sacks and a shovel and tried to get some coal for us. When they got there, sure enough there was a mountain of coal laying there inside the fence. The fence had a big hole in it and the two girls slipped in and handed out the coal to their mothers and they happily filled their sacks. All of a sudden, an American jeep came roaring up with two American soldiers with machine guns and scared the living daylights out of them. They didn't understand English, but they got the meaning "don't take any coal." They came home empty handed and very frightened. The cold was so bad that winter that the only way of being warm, was by staying in bed with blankets over you.

To see American soldiers with weapons now was very unusual. We mostly saw them driving around in their jeeps, or when they were off duty on the streetcars and also in the dance halls. Unlike Iraq, there was almost no resistance from the German people, at least not where I could see it. Once in a while, it came to a brawl with young German men and the soldiers, but that was usually because the German boys resented GIs going out with German girls. Sometimes there was graffiti on walls saying "Ami, go home." (Ami was the name the Germans called the American GIs), but otherwise things were quite peaceful. Also democracy was nothing new for Germany. We had a democracy before Hitler came to power. We were also lucky to have Konrad Adenauer, a great leader after the war, who brought Germany back again to the rest of the world. The hardworking German people also had a lot to do with the recovery, and last but not least, there was the Marshal Plan. The powers that be had realized that they couldn't treat Germany the same way as it had been treated after World War I. People have to have hope for a better future.

From 1945 to 1948, the St. Peter and Paul church services were held in a former restaurant. The ballroom was turned temporarily into our church. Then on Christmas Eve 1948, we had a big candle-light procession back to our renovated church. It seemed like all the people of Oberhausen turned out for this festive occasion. In the beginning there was standing room only in the church, as there were no benches available at that time, but we had our church back again.

1948 was the year when our money was changed over from the Reichsmark to the Deutsche Mark. Each of us received forty D Marks and was told the myth that everybody would start out equally. Of course, we were smart enough to know that there was a big difference between us and the property or factory owners, for they of course had assets and we did not. I remember my little sister was very upset. She had a small bank account, not more than twenty Reichsmark, that she had been saving for a long time. She was crying when we told her that the money was worthless. A strange thing happened after the money changing; all of a sudden you could buy things again. Food and clothing mysteriously appeared again, I don't know from where. Although things weren't by all means great, it was a beginning.

Off and on I was out of work and had to go to the unemployment office to ask if there were any jobs available. One time the lady there said she didn't have any jobs right now in my field, but there was something else that I could do. It was a job as an assistant to a magician. I told her that I had to think about it. My mother of course thought that was a bad idea, but I thought it would be kind of fun. I was just about to take the job when Mama brought in the big guns, her brother Willi. He finally succeeded in talking me out of taking the job. I always wondered what would have happened if I had taken it.

After a few jobs in different places, I was working at a place in Göggingen, a small town about 10 miles from where I lived. When the weather was nice I used my bicycle to go to work; and when it rained, I used the streetcar. My boss, Mr. Kranzfelder, was a member of the original freedom group that saved the city from final destruction. During the war, all private cars were confiscated. He however had hidden his car during that time and then used it to drive some of the other members of the freedom group to the outskirts of Augsburg to negotiate a surrender. While I was working at his business as a secretary/bookkeeper, he told me of his involvement with the freedom group.

Later on I got a job working as a bookkeeper in a bicycle shop. A little while back, I had taken a class in English and my boss thought I should now take some more classes. From then on, whenever an American came into the shop to buy a bicycle, they would call me to translate.

I also learned of an interesting story about my employers (husband and wife). The shop had belonged to a Jewish family before the war. The S. family bought it from them before the war and the family supposedly immigrated to America. Actually it was too late for them to leave the country and Mr. and Mrs. S. hid them in the storage area above the store until the air raid in 1944, when the upper story was completely destroyed. The couple survived and was hidden in the S. apartment until after the war, when they finally immigrated to America. I found all this out from Lisl, my coworker; she worked at the store as an apprentice during the war. She had suspected what was going on, but never told anybody until after the war.

My father had to be the very worst "do it yourselfer." We all dreaded when anything in the apartment had to be fixed. It usually turned into a disaster and we had to listen to his swearing when things went wrong, which they always did. My mother insisted on having the live-in kitchen painted every few years. This was a tremendous project (it was the time before we knew anything about acrylic paints). It involved washing the walls down with water and all sorts of things. I never really knew what all had to be done, because as soon I found out he was going to paint, Maya disappeared for the day and my mother and Gerda were left with him. When things really got bad, and they always did, he would start swearing ********************, whole trainloads full of **************. When I finally came back, the room was painted and my father was in good humor again, bragging how great a job he did on the walls. The only ones that weren't very happy about this situation were my mother and sister. They complained that I would always leave them to be my father's handmaidens, but at least it was over for now; they were glad for that until next time.

One great thing the Americans brought with them was the Big Band sound. My friend Anni and I just loved to dance to it. Whenever we got together at her place or mine, we would practice all the different dances and on the weekend we went dancing. We always kept track of the best bands and followed them around. We preferred to go solo; that way we could always dance with the best dancers. Everybody knew who the best dancers were, boys and girls alike. A lot of times we went outside of Augsburg to Hammel; they started the dance Sunday afternoon. We had to take the train at 1:30 PM to get there. Our main meal on Sunday was always at noon. My mother always made me do the dishes and sweep the floor before I could leave. I really tried to hurry everything along and sometimes I had to run all the way to the train station to catch the train, but I never missed it. The dance lasted until 11:30 PM, when a bus came and brought everybody back to Augsburg. However, my girlfriend and I had to be home by 10 PM, so we had to walk to Neusäss which is about halfway between Hammel and Augsburg. This was of course very unwise of our parents, just us two girls walking, sometimes at night, a few miles to the train station in Neusäss. It was too bad that a terrible thing happened to me shortly thereafter that made my parents realize it was safer to go home with the crowd on the bus.

I remember one time I didn't feel so good, but was hiding it, because I still wanted to go dancing. The next day I really felt bad and I remember leaning on the stove and my parents telling me, it was no wonder I felt so bad, dancing all day with nothing to eat (which of course was true) and the next thing I remember was me laying in bed. They told me I fainted and fell flat on the floor. Even the downstairs neighbor came up to find out what happened, because it made so much noise. I thought to myself, I bet now they are sorry for bawling me out. This was the first and only time I ever fainted in my life (at least up to now, at age seventy-five).

I am very reluctant to write about this next terrible incident. But since it is my life story, I will have to write about it. When I was around seventeen years old, a German handicapped man, who had only one leg, persuaded me to help him to carry some packages to a warehouse in a remote area. (At that time, young girls were not warned to never go with any strangers). I knew these warehouses existed, since we had them where I worked. Of course he was lying to me and all of a sudden he grabbed me, threw me to the ground and tied up my wrists at knife point. I was so scared, I thought I was going to die and started to pray out loud. My prayers were answered. Somehow this must have gotten to him, because all of a sudden he untied me and let me go. Instead of going to the next police station, I walked all the way home. My parents were very worried about me since I didn't come home at the regular time and it was dark by now. After I told them what had happened to me, and my mother and I had a good cry, we decided to go to the police station the next day. At the police station they first didn't believe me, and then the Inspector came out of his office. He took over and told the officers, "Just look at her wrists." He tried for a long time to find the perpetrator; however he was never found.

My girlfriend Anni and I loved dancing so much that Saturday and Sunday just weren't enough for us. We wanted to go on Wednesday too. The only way we could do that was to say we are going to each other's houses. Nobody had telephones at the time, so there was no way to check up on us. Anni lived about two blocks away from me. We would meet halfway, run past the intersection by our homes, make sure nobody was looking out the window and go on to the streetcar. We never did get caught.

By 1949 my girlfriend and I had a falling out. She now had a boyfriend that I didn't like. Had he been a nice guy, I would have been happy for her. Many years later, I found out that Anni had committed suicide when she was in her twenties. That was so hard for me to believe; she was always such a happy girl when I knew her.

I now went dancing with another girl I knew. Helene was the daughter of our seamstress. She was two years younger than I. She also could sew and outdistanced her mother by far. You could describe to her or show her a picture in a magazine of how you would like a dress to look, and she would make it. She never used a pattern; she only needed to take your measurements. The only problem was that she lived far away from me. She used to live close by, but since she and her family had been bombed out during the war, she lived across town now. We didn't have a telephone (this time it was to our disadvantage) so we did run into difficulties getting together.

American troops entering Augsburg April 28, 1945.
Photo by Heinz Glässel, appeared in Augsburger Allgemeine April 28, 1995.

Augsburg now

A NEW DIRECTION IN MY LIFE

On June first, 1950, I attended English class at the America Haus. Once, after class, a girl asked me to go downtown with her. She was going to buy a pair of shoes the next day and wanted to go window shopping with me, since all stores were closed already. As we walked and looked in the windows, we noticed that an American car with two soldiers inside was following us. We pretended we didn't notice, but they kept on following us. When there was traffic behind them, they had to go around the block and then they were there again. We walked down the whole stretch of town, all the way to the train station, and they continued to follow and try to talk to us. Now it became intriguing. We finally stopped and talked to them. They invited us to go for a ride with them, but since we didn't quite trust them, we said we would come along if both of us could sit in the backseat, which we did. They took us to a local Gasthaus for drinks. So when they asked me what I wanted, I said "I want some ham and eggs." I was working all day and afterwards went to English class and had nothing to eat all day. The driver of the car, his name was Toby, was very surprised that I didn't want anything to drink, but I did get my ham and eggs. Afterwards they drove us home. This is how I met my husband to be. Of course, at the time I had no idea of what the future would hold. From then on, Toby wanted to see me every day. In the beginning I didn't agree to it, but he was very persistent and I finally took him home to meet my family. Everybody liked him right away, even my grandmother and my Uncle Willi. They said, "He is just like us, not like a typical American soldier at all."

From then on we met almost every day. He usually picked me up from work and we would eat at the PX or at the Gasthaus "Black Eagle" in Kriegshaber. Maria, the daughter of the owner, dated a fellow that was in the band with Toby. His name was Patno, and we would go out on double dates with them. Patno was a real musician; I have never known anybody that could play the piano like he did. Although Toby loved the Big Band music, he didn't like to dance, which I just couldn't understand.

On weekends, Toby and I would sometimes drive to Garmisch or Berchtes-gaden in the Alps. We also went to the Oktoberfest in Munich. It was great that Toby had a car because I got to go to a lot of places that I had only heard of. (Very few people had cars at that time and during the war, traveling was very restricted). Several times we went to the opera together. I was glad that Toby and I liked classical and many other kinds of music. To see "Aida" at the Augsburg Freihlichtbühne (outdoor theater) was something to remember. The background for the theater was the over 1,000 year old walls. When there was a performance, they closed the street that led through one of the original town entrances. When they played the entrance march (from Aida), there was a fantastic procession of horses, chariots and people coming through the gate and down the street to the theater. It was very impressive.

By Christmas I thought for sure that I would get an engagement ring. How-ever, that didn't happen; instead he gave me a new bicycle. I was very disap-pointed, but didn't show it. On New Year's Eve, we went to the little town of Friedberg to a big party, and it was there that he proposed to me. I hadn't expected it then and I asked him if he had too much to drink which he hadn't. He was dead sober and dead serious. I finally did believe him and after a few days we had a small engagement party at my home.

Everything was going great. We were both very happy. We couldn't get married right away, because the rules at that time were that an American soldier could not apply for permission to marry a German girl until two months before he finished his tour of duty in Germany. However, everything changed for us when in April, 1951, Toby got orders that would transfer him to Korea (where a war was going on at that time). We applied for permission to get married, but there was not enough time to complete the necessary paperwork. Toby left one week later. He had been put on "operation pipeline," which was created to send troops from Europe to Korea. Luckily the Army Band in Georgia had a request in for a Supply Sergeant. Toby was taken off the pipe line to Korea and sent to the 336th Army Band in Camp Gordon, Georgia, which came as a complete and happy surprise to him and of course to me too. We promised to write each other every day, which we did.

Time went by and we hadn't heard anything from the Army about our mar-riage papers. I tried from my side and Toby tried from his, but nothing hap-pened. I used to go to the Kaserne (army base) inquiring about our papers, but the Sergeant there always told me that there was nothing happening. One day at the end of November I was at the Kaserne again, arguing with the Sergeant, when the Colonel in charge came out of his office and wanted to know what was going on. I told him that my fiancé and I have been waiting for over eight months for our marriage papers to come back. He then told me to come to his office and he introduced himself. His name was Colonel Buck. We had something in common right away, when I told him my name was Buk, without the C. I also told him that everybody wrote my name wrong, they always wrote it Buck. After a while he said "I don't want to be cruel, but have you considered the possibility that your fiancé changed his mind after he got back to the States?" I was ready for him; I opened my purse and took out Toby's last letter. I always put numbers on the envelopes, and that one happened to be number 202. I showed him the letter and asked him "will that convince you?" It sure did. He went out the door and told the Sergeant "you WILL look for those papers until you find them." Sure enough, he found them, already filed under "inactive." The Colonel got real mad at the Sergeant and said to me that he would do everything to start things rolling. He kept his promise and soon after I was asked to have a medical examination. Also the CID (Criminal Investigation Division) went to my neighbors, and the people I worked for and with, to inquire about my character. They also asked them of their opinion of Toby and they were all positive in their answers.

By the beginning of the year 1952, we received permission to get married. Toby applied for a furlough to return to Germany to get married. This was granted, though Toby had to sign a statement that he had enough money to pay his own way to and from Germany.

On February 25th, he left for Augsburg. He took all the money he had been saving, about 700 dollars, and went to the nearest air force base to start "hitching rides" from base to base and hopefully all the way to Germany. He made it as far as Westover Field, Mass. where he was continuously "bumped" from flights by those of higher rank. Finally, he was told by a friendly Air Force Sergeant that he had just been bumped by a Lieutenant's two dogs, and really he didn't have much chance of getting a plane. Time was running out and he had had enough. So on February 28th he took a bus to La Guardia Airport in New York, and bought a one way ticket to Frankfurt, Germany for 500 dollars. Now he had no money to get back with. He had hoped that he could make it back to me by my birthday, February 26th 1952, but he was three days late. I did receive a dozen of red roses and a phone call on my birthday from him.

We didn't have much time to plan the wedding, but on March 8th, 1952, we got married. Lilacs had always been my favorite flowers. Toby wanted me to have white lilacs for my wedding bouquet. It was still winter and lilacs weren't easy to find, but he did find them for me. We had the civil ceremony at Augsburg City Hall, with my father as best man, and then we had our wedding picture taken in downtown Augsburg. Afterwards, we had a church wedding at a Protestant church, which was kind of awkward for my whole family; especially my grandmother .Toby insisted that we not get married in a Catholic church, although I attended church at St. Peter and Paul in Oberhausen my whole life. I felt at that time since Toby had no one in his family here at our wedding, I should agree to the one request he made. I did regret it later on. We had our reception at the Gasthaus Mohrenkopf in Oberhausen. It was a great wedding. My girlfriend Helene had designed and made my wedding dress for me and gave it to me as a wedding gift. It was a beautiful dress. Our daughter Susie wore that same dress at her own wedding.

We never had a honeymoon, since Toby's leave was running out. We took the train to Frankfurt where Toby hoped to hitch a ride on a military plane back to the States. When this didn't happen, I went back to Augsburg and he took a train to Bremerhaven. There, on one of the last days of his furlough, when he should have reported back in to Camp Gordon Georgia, he went to the commanding officer in charge of the military port of Bremerhaven, a colonel. Toby told him of his situation (out of time and money) and the reasons why. The colonel was very sympathetic and said he would get him on the next troop transport back to the USA, which would be in twelve days. Then he said, "Why don't you send for your wife, and I will give you passes until the ship leaves." This was great, and we did just that. On the 21st of April, 1952, the "USNS General Alexander Patch" left Bremerhaven for the USA. It took 11 days to get to the states, which gave him lots of time to worry about his fate.

When Toby arrived in New Jersey, two MPs escorted him to the Fort Dix Provost Marshal's office where he was given a train ticket to Augusta, Ga. When he reported in at Camp Gordon, he found that he had a new band leader who welcomed him back and congratulated him on his marriage. Toby thought this was too good to be true and spent weeks, then months waiting for the ax to fall. Since he had not received any new orders on the ship, he didn't know at the time that the new C. O. had extended his furlough time and that he had been covered at all times.

While this was going on for Toby, I was waiting for my visa to come through. I had to have another medical examination and an x-ray. The Army gave me some more headaches when they told me that the x-ray showed that I had spots on my lungs and therefore they couldn't give me a visa. I immediately went to my own doctor and he told me that was ridiculous, spots on the lungs meant that my body fought off whatever illness I had had in the past. He gave me a letter to give to the military doctor and three months later, I finally got my visa. The Army would have paid for my trip to the USA, but who knows how long I would have to wait again, so we decided to pay for the trip ourselves.

Maya and Toby's wedding picture

My sister Gerda, Mama and Papa

COMING TO AMERICA

It was really hard to say goodbye to my family, not knowing when I would see them again. Toby had promised my parents that I would be back for a visit in five years. I remember when I was a little girl that a certain song would always make me cry. The song went like this: "Vogerl flieg in'd Welt hinaus, lasst dei Mutterl alleinig z'haus." It was about a little bird that flies out into the world and leaves his mother alone at home. I used to say to my mother, "This will not happen to us because I will never leave you." Well, the time had come when I did just that.

I purchased a ticket on the SS Veendam and I went first by train to Rotterdam, then on by ship to New York. On the train, I met a couple from Holland and when the train stopped in Cologne, I stepped out of the train to buy a magazine. As I was paying for the magazine, I saw the train pulling out of the station. I was frantic; all my belongings were in the train and if I missed that train I also would miss the boat. However, the train came right back. It was just changing tracks, what a relief!!

It was quite an adventure for me to be on a big ocean liner. Lots of people got sick, but it didn't bother me at all. I enjoyed all the good food. It took us eight days until we finally arrived in New York late in the afternoon. We had to stay on the ship until the next morning. Everybody was so excited; I don't think anybody went to sleep at all that night. We could see the city at night from the ship. In the morning Toby, his mother, his sister Dorrit and her husband "V'" were waiting for me as I got off the ship. We took a small tour of New York and went up in the Empire State Building. I was duly impressed with this great city. The family had all come by car and we drove back to Michigan, where Toby's father and his brother Ronnie were waiting for us. Everybody was so good to me; they treated me right away like one of the family. They had a little wedding party planned for us and even had a wedding cake. There was a reason for us coming to Michigan; the family wanted me to know what Michigan would be like. Just in case I didn't like Georgia, I would always know that Michigan would eventually be my home.

After a few days in Grand Rapids, Toby and I were on our way to Camp Gordon, Georgia. Toby had a 1941 Chrysler Crown Imperial, a huge black car. When I sat in it, I almost disappeared, and that's how big it was. We drove through Ohio, Kentucky, Tennessee, and North and South Carolina. I was so impressed with the beauty of some of the southern states, especially Kentucky and Tennessee. We finally arrived in Augusta, Georgia and nearby Camp Gordon. What really surprised me here in Georgia was the red dirt. This was new to me, since I had never seen red dirt before.

A few months before my arrival, Dorrit, "V" and Ronnie had delivered, to Georgia, a house trailer they had fixed up in Michigan and my new home was waiting there for me. I had never seen a mobile home before, but I liked it right away; it looked real homey. There were just two things it didn't have; one was a bathroom and the other air-conditioning. I arrived in Georgia at the end of July and was it ever hot there. I never had experienced that kind of heat and humidity in Germany; it was unbearable. One time it was 120 degrees in the mobile home. There was no relief outside either and in the evening when it cooled down a little bit, all of the gnats were out and chased you back inside. Coming from very cool and temperate Germany to hot and humid Georgia was quite a shock, and there were many more to come.

I always thought I spoke English pretty well, but in Georgia I didn't understand the local people and they didn't understand me. It was like we spoke different languages and I was quite upset when they called me "honey" and they didn't even know me. When we went shopping, I let Toby do all the talking. We found a Jewish bakery in Augusta that had the type of bread that I was used to in Germany. One day the lady there said to Toby, "She sure doesn't say much." Toby told her that I had just come here from Germany, and then the woman said in the most New York Jewish accent, "Just give her time and she will talk like the rest of us."

Toby was gone quite a lot; sometimes he had to play for army events all over the state. I couldn't go with him, since I didn't drive and he had to go with the band by bus.

Reading has always been my number one hobby, but up till then all my reading had been done in German. I somehow had to learn how to read English fluently. Toby's sister Dorrit had left some Woman's Day magazines in the trailer for me. This was the beginning of my reading in English. Shortly after we moved there, Toby and I went to the library and since I liked mysteries, I started checking out the Perry Mason books by Earl Stanley Gardner. I think I probably read all the ones that were available since I didn't know any other author. I also improved my English by listening to the Arthur Godfrey Show on the radio.

Toby usually came home for lunch and sometimes we went shopping for groceries at that time. I had a little refrigerator and lots of cupboard space. One day after shopping, and after Toby went back to work, I started to put everything away. I knew what belonged in the refrigerator, but sometimes I ran into things I had never seen before. One of them was a cardboard tube of biscuits. It looked to me like it should go in the cupboard and that's where I put it. I then settled down for some reading. All of a sudden, I heard an explosion (remember it was very hot in the trailer) that seemed to come from the kitchen. When I looked in the cabinet, there was biscuit dough stuck all over the ceiling of the cabinet.

By August I was pregnant and as pregnant women everywhere know, I had to use the toilet quite a lot. Well, the toilets and washrooms were quite a distance from our trailer and sometimes Toby had to go with me in the middle of the night. When you turned on the lights, the floors came to life, as all the cockroaches ran for shelter. This was also a first for me. I had never seen cockroaches before.

Since I was now pregnant, I had to go to the military doctor. When I first got there, the nurse asked all the usual questions, USUAL for everybody else, but not for me. One of the things she asked me was "How often do you go to the bathroom?" (In Germany, a bathroom is a room with a bathtub or shower in it, everything else is a toilet). So when she asked me that question I told her "Never." I could see she was shocked by my answer and she said "What do you mean you never go to the bathroom, you must go sometimes." I said, "But I don't have a bathroom." Well, I finally figured out what she meant. When you first report to the doctor, they had a lot of pregnant women sit in a circle and a doctor would explain what to expect in your pregnancy. He said if you have any questions at all, just raise your hand and I will explain it to you. One of the things that doctor was saying that it was very important to have a regular bowel movement. I never heard that word before and since he said it was so important, I raised my hand and asked him, "What is a bowel movement?" to the laughter of the whole group. He said, "Let your husband explain it to you." Never a dull moment!!

We never had much money. Toby only got paid about 120 dollars a month. By the end of the month, we were totally broke. I had learned from my mother how to make something out of very little, and this came in handy now. However, there was never anything left for entertainment. I do remember though that one time we bought a Monopoly game with the last of our money.

In December 1952, we drove up to Grand Rapids, Michigan to spend Christmas with Toby's family. The trip up was quite stressful for me. I was now four months pregnant and was sick most of the time during the trip. My in-laws had a surprise for us; they had bought a TV set. I had never seen one before and was very impressed. We spent most of our time glued to the TV.

While living in the trailer in Georgia I did the kind of German cooking I was used to, but my mother-in-law cooked some things I had never heard of, like squash, corn on the cob, sweet potatoes and pumpkin pie. Pumpkin pie was Toby's favorite dessert and I always let him have my piece of pie until I finally tried it myself. I really liked it and decided to try some of the other things I had never had before like popcorn, olives, celery and watermelons. Most of them I liked, but to this day I still don't like celery, olives and sweet potatoes. From then on Toby didn't get my pie anymore.

People always told me that spring was the most beautiful time in Georgia with all the azaleas and rhododendrons in bloom. Well, I never did see Georgia in the spring time. Toby got discharged from the Army in February 1953.

Back: Toby's father, brother Ron & his mother. Front: Toby, Maya, sister Dorrit
& husband "V"

THE BEGINNING OF
CIVILIAN LIFE

We returned to Michigan and moved in with Toby's parents. They had fixed up a small apartment upstairs for us and on May 4, 1953, our daughter Karin Marie was born. The whole family was thrilled as she was the first grandchild in both of our families. I felt really bad that my mother couldn't be there, but my mother-in-law was a lot of help to me. As a wedding gift from Toby's parents, we had been given the adjoining lot to their property and Toby and his father started to build our very first house. They did all the work themselves, but we did have a mortgage of $6,400.

One time Toby and I were shopping at a department store in Grand Rapids, when I saw a sales girl that looked so familiar to me. She looked like someone who went to the Kapellen Schule at the same time I did. It seemed so unlikely, so I asked Toby to listen to her talk, to see if she had an accent. Sure enough, she did so I started to talk to her. Yes, she was from Augsburg. She was two grades below me in school, but she remembered me too. What a small world!! We became good friends and so did our husbands and we stayed in contact for many years. Finally in 1989, after all our moves, we lost contact and never found them again. Since their names were Rosie and Wayne Smith, it was impossible to trace them on the Internet.

At first, Toby had odds-and-ends jobs, nothing really great. So he decided to go back to school on the GI bill. When our house was finished, we finally moved in, and when Karin was nine months old, I got pregnant again. We kept it secret for a while from his family since it was so soon after Karin. We finally had to tell them because I couldn't do any more hard work in our garden. For the first time in my life, I had a real garden. It was so great to grow my own tomatoes. However, whenever there was a ripe one on the vine, my mother-in-law would bring it to me. I finally had to tell her that I wanted to pick my own tomatoes.

December 1, 1954, Kenneth T. Torngren was born. I remember celebrating Christmas in my own house with my own Christmas baby. This was a hard time for all of us. Toby was gone all of the time. During the day he went to school and at night he had a job at the grocery store for one dollar an hour. We received a little money from the government, but never enough. The Veterans Vocational school Toby went to was about forty miles away and sometimes he didn't even have enough money for gas. His mother usually would come out to give him a few dollars.

When Kenny was about six months old, we had him baptized in the Lutheran church. We had Karin along too. She was a little over two years old and had never been to church before. When the people started to sing the hymns, Karin started to sing "The yellow rose of Texas." Well, what do you expect, it was her favorite song at that time and she wanted to sing along.

Since we had very little money, I never could afford to buy much clothing for myself. My mother-in-law, and Dorrit, my sister-in-law, sewed all their own clothing and I always admired them for it since I couldn't sew. My mother-in-law then told me that she would teach me how to sew, but after I said I couldn't do it she said, "I will teach you as soon as you say to me that you CAN do it." Well, I did learn how to sew and the first thing I made was mother and daughter dresses for Karin and me. I wish Toby's mother could have lived long enough to see what I can do today with my quilting and it all started with her. I was always close to Dorrit; she was and remains a second sister to me.

It was wintertime. We had lots of snow, and one day, when Toby was at work and I was alone with the kids, suddenly Kenny stopped breathing. I wrapped him up and ran barefooted next door. Luckily, my mother-in-law knew what to do, she gave him a cool bath and he snapped out of it. This was the first time he had convulsions. He had them two more times, every time it was very scary for us.

By 1956, Toby was done with his school; he was now officially a Tool and Die Designer. He got a job in Lansing, Michigan, and in the beginning he stayed there in an apartment during the week and came home on the weekends. We finally decided that we had to move to Lansing. We sold our house for $ 10,500 and were then looking for something in Lansing. This was Michigan's capitol and homes were more expensive than they were in Grand Rapids. First we stayed in a couple of rental houses, one worse than the other. In the first one, we had a family of rats living in the basement, and the second was infested with mice. Toby went mouse hunting each evening with a jar, a stick, and some string, on our countertops in the kitchen. He really was good at it, but he could not keep up with them.

Then on a beautiful day in August 1956, while I was doing the daily chore of looking through the paper for houses for sale, one ad caught my eye. "For Sale, garage house with all the bricks to build a house on one acre lot in a beautiful subdivision." I could hardly wait for Toby to come home from work so we could go there and look at it. Before he came home, it started to rain quite hard, but a little rain couldn't dampen my curiosity a bit. So we took Karin four and Kenny almost two, to look at the house. As we drove through the subdivision we were so busy admiring all the nice houses that we passed right by without noticing it. Then the second time around—there it was—sticking out like a sore thumb, a little bit of a brick house with a big window in front and about twenty feet to one side, a frame garage. Since it was pouring by now, only Toby and I went out of the car and ran to the door, but nobody was home. We weren't going to give up that easy though. So we went all around the house and yard and right then and there I fell completely in love—not with the house—but with the lot. Here was everything I ever wanted: a large yard, trees, bushes and flowers. The look on Toby's face told me he felt the same way. When we got back to the car, we looked like a pair of drowned rats. As soon as we got home, Toby called up the real estate agent and made an appointment to see the inside of the house. It turned out to be three small rooms with a half bath. We were sold on it completely, bought it, and moved in a short time after, loaded with ideas and anxious to make them real. I remember that the neighbors were quite apprehensive as we moved in. Later we found out that we were the third set of buyers that purchased the house with the intention of building on to it, but it had always remained the same. Since it was already September there was little we could do that year.

In the fall of 1956, I applied for citizenship. I had to take a course in American Government and History. Then, on November 29, 1956 I became a proud citizen of the United States of America. It was too late for that year's election, so I had to wait four more years before I could vote for the first time.

At the time we got married, Toby had promised my parents that I would be able to come back home for a visit in five years. As things were, with a new home and also a new baby that I was expecting again in September, that promise was just about impossible to keep. So Toby asked my mother to come over here. She arrived in May, 1957. Until that time, I never knew that Toby could speak and understand so much German. It was a complete surprise to me when all of a sudden he was speaking to me and Mama like a native Augsburger. Toby told me later that this was his way to make me speak English. (Also, it was his way to listen in on what was going on around him when he was visiting at my home, that's what I think!)

At the same time, Toby started adding on to the house. We were now three adults and two children living in the little house. Things went very well through the whole summer. The house was really taking shape now. Since I was expecting in September, there wasn't any way that I could help in the actual building, but as Toby did all the work alone (except the brick-laying) there sure was a lot of holding to do. I think I must have held that whole house together at one time or another. The new house had a different roof line and we were faced with taking the roof off from over our heads. When the time finally came, things began to happen. First of all, the company Toby worked for went on overtime and there was no way for him to get out of it. That left him with almost no time at all to work on the house. The original roof was now already off and the only thing between us and the sky above was a plaster ceiling. It had been an exceptionally dry summer, excellent building weather, but September was here and it was just too good to last. On September 12, I went to the hospital and had a baby girl, Susan Marie. On September 13, it started to rain and rain and rain. That evening I could hardly wait for Toby to come and see me, so I could find out what was happening at home. But he hadn't been home since morning when he had taken the children and my mother to Grand Rapids to his parents' home. That was quite a load off my mind. At least they were safe and dry. While the people around us were chatting happily, Toby and I just sat there during the whole visiting hour, staring out the window at the rain that came pouring down.

A few days later when it was time for me to leave the hospital, Toby told me that the house would look "a little different," and it sure did. The ceiling was gone in the living room. Not until later did I find out what really happened that night. After leaving the hospital that evening on the 13th, Toby went home, unlocked the door that opened into the living room and after a few minutes, as he went to the kitchen to fix himself something to eat, there was a groaning noise and the whole living room ceiling came down. It broke an arm off the couch. If it hadn't been for tremendous luck on Toby's part, the whole thing could have turned into a tragedy. He told me later that he was quite shook up. For the longest time I had believed that the ceiling was already down when he came home that fateful night. (He didn't want to upset me).

The next day, a very good neighbor from across the street loaned us a huge tarp and he and Toby tacked it on to the roof rafters. It kept on raining for a whole week though. Water was coming in everywhere, especially in the kitchen and living room. We had jars, pails, pots and pans standing everywhere on the floor, catching the dripping water. My mother spent most of her time mopping up buckets full of water, since I wasn't in any condition to do hard work yet. There was only one place in the whole house that was completely dry, and that was a little closet where we kept the new baby.

One evening, the wind was blowing especially hard and the rain was coming down all around us. Toby was working late and everything just seemed so hopeless. When he finally came in the door he found both Mama and I sitting there on the broken couch, crying. So he said "Well, that's all we need ... more water," and we all had a much needed laugh.

Then a few days later, it finally stopped raining. Mama was a real old-fashioned German Hausfrau and as long as I can remember, Saturday was the day she washed the floors on her hands and knees and on Wednesdays they were "wished" which means they were mopped with a long-handled mop. So from the day she arrived here, she did the same thing in my house. Toby used to tease her and say that she was wearing out the floors. When Saturday came that week, she thought over the situation very carefully and then announced: "I don't think I am going to wash the floors today."

From then on, things started going better again and soon we got our new roof on. Our newborn Susie was the best baby we have ever had. She would lie in her bassinet for hours, looking up at the rafters and at the tarp that moved a little with the wind. She slept through all the hammering and sawing and it didn't bother her at all. Mama stayed with us until January 1958, we wanted her to be with us to celebrate Christmas.

In the spring of 1958, we finally moved into the addition of our house. We now had two bedrooms, a den and a full bathroom downstairs, and three bedrooms and a full bath upstairs. All the kids now had their own bedrooms, but they weren't all finished yet. Some of them had only studs for walls. I still remember that Kenny was so excited when he finally got real walls in his bedroom.

That summer, we got a basset hound named Sam. He was mainly Karin's dog. She took care of him most of the time. Sam could sense a storm coming up miles away, and just couldn't control himself when he knew what was coming. We had some big thunderstorms in Michigan and sometimes even tornados. One did strike not too far away from us.

Summers in Michigan were always very hot and humid (but not as bad as in Georgia). We didn't have air conditioning, and I didn't know anybody who did at that time. When August came around, it was canning time, and usually the hottest time of the year. There were lots of fruits and vegetables available in Michigan. You could get a bushel of peaches for three dollars and a bushel of tomatoes for two dollars, including the basket. I usually canned peaches and tomatoes. One year we were invited to dinner at a friend's house and she served very delicious dill pickles that she had canned herself. I got her recipe and decided to make some myself that year. I followed her recipe exactly and ended up with about ten quart jars of pickles. When I served them to my family, they didn't say they liked them, but they also didn't say that they didn't. However the pickles disappeared real fast, so I assumed that they really liked them. The next year I told Toby since everybody liked my pickles so much, I was going to make some more. So Toby had to tell me what actually happened to my pickles. Every time he went to the dump he took one jar of pickles with him and threw them out, jar and all. He didn't have the heart to tell me that those pickles were awful, but couldn't take the chance that I would make some more. I have never canned any pickles since that time. Toby liked the job that he had at that time and things were going very well for us. Around this time, I took a drivers education class and received my first driver's license.

In October 1959, I was pregnant again with my fourth child. Unfortunately the company that Toby was working for went out of business and he lost his job. He then worked odd jobs here and there for a while. One of the jobs was working for a contractor as a carpenter. He was working on a second story scaffold when it broke and Toby fell to the ground breaking his left arm. When he tried to collect his unemployment money, he was told, since he broke his arm, that he was no longer available for work, so no unemployment money. This was quite a blow for us. Here we were a family with three children and one on the way and no money coming in. He finally convinced the unemployment office, that since he broke his left arm, he was still able to do his work as a Designer with his right arm.

Since I had three children in five years, I didn't really have any time to get home-sick. However, every Christmas I missed my family and Germany very much. It started in November when I heard "Silent Night" played in the stores. Every time I heard that song, I started to cry. That was very embarrassing for me, with the shoppers staring at me, wondering what was the matter with me. It took many years before I could listen to "Silent Night" without getting very emotional about it.

In June 1960, Susie was playing with the rest of the neighborhood kids across the street at a neighbor's big playground. She was hit in the face by one of the heavy metal swings. Her face was covered with blood and we rushed her to Sparrow hospital. It was sheer panic for us; Toby was also worried about me since I was almost full-term pregnant. We found out that Susie's nose was very badly smashed and the Doctors there had to completely reconstruct her nose. They really did a wonderful job.

On July 18, 1960, I had a little boy. We named him Gary T. While I was in the hospital, Toby brought me raspberries every day. They were in season and he knew how much I liked them. (I still do). Susie just loved her little brother and was very protective of him all during their childhood.

In November 1960, I voted for the first time as an American citizen. Since coming to the U.S., I considered myself a Democrat. So my very first vote went to John F. Kennedy. When he won, I even sent congratulations to the White

House and did receive an answer. We all were so enthusiastic about our new, young President.

Toby finally got a job with Reo Motors in Lansing and then with Mitchell Bentley in Ionia. I was driving now and could get out of the house sometimes by myself. One time, while shopping in Grand Ledge (a little town outside of Lansing) I met Barbara Floeter, a girl from Berlin, Germany. Through her I joined the Overseas Wives Club in Lansing. We met once a month and had a party with our husbands on Valentines Day and Halloween. We always had a lot of fun and made lots of friends. We had one girl from England and one from India; the rest of the girls were from Germany.

In the beginning of 1962, Toby's mother was ill for a very short time and died in the hospital after an operation. It was very sad for me; I really loved her very much. This really made it very important to me to think about going back to see my family. One never knows what's going to happen in the future. I had now lived in America for ten years, and it was time for me to go back for a visit. In May, 1962 I took Susie, (four) and Gary (almost two) on the trip back home. We used the most inexpensive airline which was "Luxemburg Airlines."

It was no easy task to travel with two small children. We went from Detroit to New York, to Revjajik, Iceland. There we had a layover because something was wrong with the plane. They put everybody up in a hotel and also gave us a bus tour of the town and showed us some of the hot springs, which were very interesting. I stayed on the bus most of the time; it was too hard to cope with the two children. Since it was close to Solstice, it never really got dark there. The next day, it was on to Luxemburg and then to Frankfurt where we had to stay overnight once more. The next morning at the train station Susie got really sick to her stomach and I took her to the bathroom. There, the bathroom matron stood in front of the stall and said "Not in my toilet." I pushed her aside and told her to get out of my way. Boy was I mad!! I guess the mother hen instinct was taking over. We finally made it on to our train. A few hours later we arrived in Augsburg where my family was waiting for us at the train station.

Susie and Gary were spoiled by all my relatives. Since Papa was surrounded by girls all his life (three sisters, two daughters and three granddaughters), he really enjoyed getting to know one of his grandsons. One time we went to the Plärrer and we had to walk quite a while to get there. Susie couldn't understand why nobody had a car. She said to my father, "Why can't we take a taxi?" He thought that was very funny. (The only time my father ever took a taxi was at my wedding). Susie also got along with the neighbor kids; the language barrier didn't bother her at all. Except one time a boy hit her with something and we asked why he did it. He answered, "I told her to get out of the way (of course, in German), but she didn't listen." All too soon the time was over and we had to leave. When Toby picked us up in Detroit, he was driving an awful Volkswagen Bus that he bought while we were gone.

Between 1962 and 1964, Toby worked at Oldsmobile. While he was working there, they had some very nice Christmas parties that included the wives. Toby introduced me to some of his co-workers at our table. He told them that I was originally from Germany, so one of the men asked me what town I lived in. I told him that I lived in Augsburg and that my home town was destroyed on my fifteenth birthday the night of February 25/26, 1944. There was a long pause. Finally he said, "I was in one of the planes that night when we bombed Augsburg." It was real strange to meet someone that had been involved in the bombing and could have been responsible for the deaths of my family and me. He was a real nice person, a Canadian, and I liked him right away. I think it shook him up too. It showed once again to me how senseless war was and still is.

While Toby was working at Oldsmobile, he had the opportunity to buy surplus upholstery material. I used one remnant, it was a beautiful light green embossed material, and made a cocktail dress for myself. Luckily at that time the "shift" was in fashion, which meant it was very easy to make. I wore it for the first time to the company Christmas party. As we were sitting around the table, Toby accidentally spilled a whole glass of red wine on my dress. A guy he worked with said to him, "Boy, are you going to get it when you get home, ruining your wife's new dress." I just got up and said, "No problem," the wine ran right off my dress without staining it. Of course, the material was meant for cars and was highly stain resistant. Everybody was just so amazed. I guess nobody ever thought of making a dress out of the car upholstery fabric and I wasn't going to tell them. Toby wasn't very happy at Oldsmobile and after two years he went back to Mitchell Bently in Ionia.

Now that I was a driver, I sometimes drove down to Grand Rapids to visit Dorrit, Toby's sister. I remember that I was driving a Pontiac Tempest convertible at the time. I had decided to take all the kids to Grand Haven, Michigan, which was on the shore of Lake Michigan. Dorrit and her kids (Doug and Patti) and I with our kids (Karin, Kenny, Susie and Gary)—all six kids and two mothers in an open convertible with no seatbelts. (Cars didn't have seatbelts at that time.) The kids were having such great fun and were standing up in the car while I was driving. I finally had to stop the car and threaten them to behave or we would return again to town. I shiver today at the thought of six kids in that convertible.

Our subdivision was called "Greenfield Acres" because the lots were all one acre in size. There were no fences in between the lots; everything was open. The only fence was in the back; it separated the "Dawn Haven" subdivision from ours. At the end of our road, there was some open space, mostly woods. Sometimes Paula, a neighbor and friend, and I took the neighborhood kids on a little hike through the woods. That always was lots of fun for everybody, except that the mosquitoes tried to eat us alive. On one of the days, we were ready to go, I could smell something really strong, so I said to Paula "I see you are prepared for the mosquitoes." She smiled and said "This is not mosquito spray I am wearing, it is my perfume." So much for that!! Greenfield Acres was a great place for kids to grow up. It was a time when kids could stay kids for a long time.

We were the first family in the neighborhood to have a color TV set. All the kids' friends wanted to come over and see it. One time we saw the boy that lived in back of us, looking through the fence, trying to see our color TV.

We used to get together with my friend Jo Ann Hull and her kids. We had planned a cook-out for the weekend, so Jo Ann and I drove in to Lansing to buy some steaks. It was November 23, 1963. That's when we heard that President Kennedy had been shot. I will add here an essay that I wrote January 1964:

Lansing, Michigan, January 4, 1964
On the death of our beloved President

What does it feel like to lose a great man? When you first heard about it, you tried desperately to tell yourself, "It isn't true—it can't be true; any minute now you will find out that it was just a nightmare." But deep in the back of your mind, you know it happened and everything about it is just like they are telling you right in front of you on the TV screen. You hurt so bad, deep down in your heart and also right above your throat, and when it is time to eat, the lump in your throat won't move and you can hardly swallow.

After this first numbness come the questions. Why did he have to die? A brilliant man in the prime of his life, loved by millions all over the world, dedicated to peace and freedom, dedicated to the well-being of all people, rich or poor, black or white. Why him? Oh God help me understand your ways. You see the hurt in the people's faces; everybody is so so sad … and you hear it over and over again, "It feels like I have lost someone in my own family" 99% of America felt that way. But then you raise the question: How could that horrible thing happen in America, a civilized country? And then comes the reckoning … It comes home with your children from school, when they tell you with tears in their eyes and anger in their faces: "Did you hear what happened, they shot our president and do you know what some of them (the children) said: "I hope he dies." It comes home when you read in an editorial about some anonymous phone calls several papers got in the south: "So they killed the n***** lover, good for the one who did it." And there you have your 1%. The people who still call themselves Americans, although I think they have no right doing so. When hate is so embedded in the human mind that there is room for nothing else, it is a sad, sad thing. This kind of hate inside a country is what cancer is inside the body. It has to be stopped before it is too late.

Many people have been saying: "there are so few that feel that way." Yet it took only one man and two bullets to kill our beloved President.

As I was watching (on television) the caisson with the body of President Kennedy come down Pennsylvania Avenue and heard a band play America the beautiful, I felt like crying out: "Oh America, my adopted country that I love so very much—today you aren't so beautiful."

Since then, Christmas has come and gone, and so has New Year's Day. It hasn't been the same as in past years. It seems something inside of us has died also, that November day in Dallas.

Many have paid tribute to the late president by naming places all over the world after him. President Kennedy showed us what he would do for his country—he died for it. Let us Americans pay a living tribute to him by showing the world what we can do for our country and let us begin by joining together and pledging anew "Allegiance to the Flag of the United States of America and to the Republic for which it stands, one Nation, under God, with Liberty and Justice for all" and this time—like President Kennedy wrote in his Thanksgiving message, which he never delivered—"Let us not utter words, but let us live by them."

Maria Torngren
January 4, 1964

In 1965, Mama came to visit us again. This time we had a big house and she had her own room. The kids really enjoyed being with her and had lots of fun with her, even though she couldn't speak any English. One of the first words she learned was "sale." She always pointed that out to me when she saw it in the paper. We had some funny things happen with her. One time we all went shopping and Mama stayed home. A friend of Toby's had called to ask if he could borrow our lawn mower. So we explained to her, that if a young man comes to the door, you let him take the lawn mower. When we came back, Mama said, the man came, but he didn't want to take the lawn mower. We didn't at first know what was happening, until we got a phone call from one of Toby's other friends and he said "I stopped by at your house today, but you weren't home and your mother-in-law absolutely wanted me to take a lawn mower. I kept telling her, I don't want a lawn mower, but she was very persistent. I finally managed to get away without the mower."

My mother always tried everything, even things she didn't know. (I think she was sure that she would never have to see dog meat again). One time she opened a package of dog food and tried it and the kids said, "No Oma, you can't eat that, that's dog food, food for Hunde (dogs)". Another time, we had stopped and picked up some take out food from "Dogs and Suds." When we brought it home, Mama said she didn't want anything, when we asked why not, she said "It says right here on the bag that it is for dogs."

Mama was here for at least six months. Shortly after she got back to Germany, my father was diagnosed with lung cancer and died soon after. My father never got to meet Karin and Kenny.

In 1965, Toby had to work overtime constantly. The kids and I very seldom saw him any more. He was gone all the time. About that time we had a visit from Rosie and Wayne, who were here on vacation in Michigan. Wayne now worked with the American Army in Germany. They really liked staying over there and told us to try to do the same. We talked it over and decided to sell our house and move to Europe. It looked like we would be ready to move by December. Then we thought, why go to Europe in the winter time. We might as well take a vacation in a warm climate. We thought of many places we could go to, but finally decided on the Canary Islands. Then we started looking into how we would get there.

We sold our house just before Halloween and attended the combination Halloween Party and goodbye party that the Overseas Wives Club held for us. Toby was working so hard on his costume all day that he even forgot to eat. He was going as a Viking. The party was the Saturday after Halloween and it was quite cold and snowing outside. Toby with his Viking helmet, barefoot with sandals, rang the doorbell at the house where we thought the party was; however, it was the wrong house, so we got some strange looks from the people living there. We finally got to the right house and had a great time for a while. Toby had a few drinks on an empty stomach, and to make a long story short, we never made it to dinner. Our friends Kenny and Rennie Raymont helped me take him home. The kids were worried when they saw us helping Toby in; they thought something bad happened to him. I told them "he just had a little too much to drink."

Greenfield Acres (Lansing, Michigan) house: Before

Greenfield Acres house: Finished

Oma and her grandkids

From left: Karin, Kenny, Susie and Gary

Torben the Viking with Ursula

OUR ONCE IN A LIFE TIME TRIP

After checking, it looked like a freighter would be the most economical way to go to North Africa. So we booked passage on the Yugoslavian freighter "Visavica."

Just at that time, Toby was offered a job with Mack Western Trucks in Hayward, California, but since all the arrangements were already made for our trip; he had to turn it down. Sometimes we think how different things could have been if we had moved to California then.

Before we left on our trip, we had a talk with all the kids' teachers. We were told to make sure to take along a lot of books for them to read. The trip itself would be a great learning experience for them. Karin was very unhappy to leave all her friends and her dog Sam. During the trip she made a list of all the things she missed. She wrote this list on January 2, 1967, just 21 days after we had left. She was not very happy.

Things I miss: January 2nd, 1967

1) Sam	10) Lansing	19) Our telephone
2) MY friends	11) Michigan	20) AMERICAN food
3) MY relatives	12) U.S.A.	21) going shopping
4) OUR house	13) OUR yard	22) football games
5) MY school	14) Most of our neighbors	23) US movies
6) MY section	15) OUR TV shows	24) basketball games
7) MY classes	16) MY ROOM	25) Christmas tree
8) MY teachers	17) OUR furniture	26) snow
9) Greenfield acres	18) MY books	27) slumber parties

28) staying over-night

29) SCHOOL parties

30) American songs

31) American radio stations

32) TV

33) going to the library with L.S.

34) Grand Ledge

35) Grand Rapids

36) hard water

37) TV commercials

38) bath tubs

39) US toilet paper

40) not being stared at

41) US music

42) informal eating

43) arguing with Millie

44) wearing cutoffs

45) not being so polite all the time

46) report cards

47) tests

48) mail

49) department stores

50) HOME in Greeenfield Acres

51) grocery stores

52) EVERYTHING

Around this time, the song "Moon River" by Andy Williams was very popular, it became our song; "six drifters off to see the world, there's such a lot of world to see." We were off to do just that.

We finally had all our packing done and on December 12, 1966 we left for New York in our brand new Dodge van. Since we thought we would be staying in Europe for several years, we took along a lot of "stuff." We even had to rent a small trailer for our belongings. On December 16, we left New York on the Yugoslavian freighter "Visavica" for Tangier, Morocco.

We had all different types of people as our fellow passengers, from English globetrotters, some Yugoslavian people, to a lot of beatniks. We even had a professional American cartoonist on board who gave Gary his latest book about a "Jewish Batman," really funny. One evening I talked to an older Yugoslavian woman. She told me that the people at her table at dinner time were admiring our family, such nice and well behaved children, and she also said that I looked like their older sister. How about that!!

On Christmas Eve we were getting close to land. The crew had been very good to us. The head waiter, whose name was Mario, had taken a real liking to the kids and kept them well supplied with oranges, apples, grapes, bananas, cookies etc. etc. during the whole trip. We took pictures of him and the kids with the Polaroid camera and gave him a copy. He was really pleased about it. The Polaroid was a great friend maker and ice breaker throughout the whole trip. On Christmas Eve the crew went all out to give us a nice Christmas Dinner. There were balloons for the kids and a bar of marzipan for me on the dinner table. After dinner, Santa Claus came to our cabin. We had little gifts stashed away for the kids. After a while, the ship's Doctor came to our cabin and wanted to take pictures of us. We had a Christmas tree and stars that we had made out of paper, hanging from the ceiling. He would have liked so much to hear us sing "Stille Nacht" (Silent Night), but the kids were too shy. After a while, we all went up to the lounge. Everybody was there, the passengers and quite a few of the crew. We sang, drank, and had a good time. One of the officers and the bartender played guitars. The crew was not allowed to join in any Christmas carols but we sure had a lot of fun and it was about 2 AM before we went to bed. Karin went down to the cabin with Gary at about midnight, but Susie and Kenny stayed to the very end.

We got up real early in the morning (it sure was a short night) and went out on deck and there it was … Africa, all red from the rising sun. What a sight!! Somehow I expected to see flat land, but there were mountains everywhere. After breakfast, we started to get ready to leave the ship. We anxiously watched our car get unloaded. An old Arab with a long robe and beard was directing the crane, but everything went alright. We finally got off the ship, crammed everything into our car, including the kids and a young Arabian boy named Riff. He was going to be our guide. Riff directed us to our hotel. How we ever made it up there I will never know. The streets were so narrow and steep, and with all the people, donkeys and carts, there was hardly any room for cars, especially a big American van. At one time, the van touched the curb on both sides. After we checked into our hotel, Toby drove the car to the English garage and left it there. Riff, our guide took us around the Casbah, the market, and all through the Arabian Quarter. It was such an unusual sight: the men in their long robes, the women with their veils, and everybody wanted to sell you something. We bought a few items and quickly found out that you never pay the first price they asked of you. Our hotel, the Hotel Continental, had quite a view and must have been at one time the best hotel in Tanger. We saw pictures of old movie stars on the walls. We were just about the only guests there, and they tried real hard to please us. They even asked us what they should cook for us. Toby had heard about couscous and sure enough, we got it for lunch. The kids weren't very thrilled about it and didn't eat very much of it. The next day Riff showed us the European section of town, there it looked like a typical European town, and you couldn't tell that you were in Africa.

The next morning we picked up our car and left Tanger (Tangier). We drove through beautiful mountainous countryside, through Tetouan, a town with all white buildings and palm trees in the middle of the mountains, then on to Ceuta, where we caught a boat to Spain. We passed right by the Rock of Gibraltar and arrived in Algeciras, Spain.

We were now on our way to Cadiz, Spain. We were again driving through mountains and later stopped at a motel/hotel type of place in Tarifa, the "Meson de Sancho" for the night. Our hotel was beautifully located on a hill with a terraced garden and a patio surrounded by orange trees. Coming from Michigan, we had never seen oranges growing on trees before. We made a new friend there; his name was Fernando. He spoke English quite well, which helped an awful lot.

In the morning, we went for a walk up the mountain side. What a beautiful sight it was! All the mountains and valleys were gorgeous, and as a bonus, you could see the Mediterranean and Africa on the other side. It was kind of hard to get down the mountain again. We met a shepherd about halfway down who directed us toward the best place to get down again. He shook his head as he watched me coming down. I guess Senoras don't go mountain climbing there, only "crazy tourista."

We liked it so much there in Tarifa that we decided to stay a few more days. One evening a group of Spanish boy scouts were showing movies at our hotel and the Boy Scout leader was very pleased to hear that Kenny had been a boy scout too. It was very interesting, especially since we didn't speak Spanish and he didn't speak English.

It was finally time to move on. Karin took pictures of Fernando, the maid and her daughter with her Swinger camera. They were so pleased. This camera was sure a lot of fun, a real friend maker. We then started our drive to Cadiz with everybody's good wishes. When we arrived in Cadiz, we bought our tickets for the ship to the Canary Islands. We had a real good lunch at an outdoor restaurant. What was so interesting about this restaurant was that the waiters had to run back and forth across a busy street to serve the people who wanted to eat in the sun, at the edge of a park, which was across the street from the restaurant. Their men's bathroom kept the boys in stitches for the next few hours. Kenny absolutely had to draw me an exact illustration of the men's room, which consisted of two holes in the floor and that's all there was to it.

After customs and everything else, it was time to board the ship. It was New Year's Eve, but not much was happening on board. The food was very good, six courses every time, lunch and dinner, and it was a surprise every time, since we couldn't read the menu. One time we had fish as the second course, which is nothing unusual, but when the fish, with his eyes open, lies on your plate with his own tail in his mouth, that's another story. To make things even worse, the radio was playing opera music and a woman was singing an aria. When Karin opened and closed the mouth of the fish with her knife, it gave the appearance that the fish was doing the singing. We all just broke up with laughter.

In January 1967, we finally saw land. The first sight of a volcanic island is really something. It is just a huge mountain range sticking out of the water. As you get closer you can see the black, red and white beaches and more greenery than we expected, mainly banana trees, cactus and pine trees. We decided to get off at the first island, which was Tenerife. We spent two nights in hotels, while we looked for a house to rent. We found a three-bedroom house halfway up the mountain, overlooking Santa Cruz in a section called "Vista Bella" (beautiful view), and it was.

After we moved into our rented house (amongst the locals), our kids started playing outside with the immediate neighbors' kids. So when the ice cream man came around on his tricycle, Toby bought ice cream for all the kids. From then on, every day there were more and more children for Toby to buy ice cream for, which was alright with him, as the ice cream was very inexpensive.

During our month in Tenerife, we covered most of the island. The roads here were wild, up, down and around. We had never seen anything like it anywhere. Everybody tooted their horns on every curve, just in case, because there is just enough room for two cars to pass by each other. (In some places there is only room for one car, and you take your turn.) We never got used to hearing a blast of horn and then seeing a Greyhound size bus coming around the sharp curves at us. We knew there was not enough room left for us, but somehow we always made it.

We were so impressed with the beautiful flowers everywhere. You could drive for miles with poinsettias as big as small trees on the side of the road. On one occasion, we decided to go and look at a beach where we could go swimming. Well, it turned out to be a big nothing. So "old map reader first class" Toby decided to take a shortcut over to another scenic mountain. The road widths on our map are designated by different colors, white, being the narrowest. We had never been on a "white" road before, so our shortcut would be our first try. These mountain roads are wild anyway; there are no guard rails, except in a few, very few places on the newer roads. In 99% of the places, there is just the edge of the road, and thousands of feet of nothing till the bottom—. Back to the short-cut—The road started out OK but the higher we went, the narrower the road got. Then the pavement ended. Toby wanted to turn around, but there wasn't enough room. So on we went. It finally got down to one lane (a Volkswagen lane). I was scared stiff and I kept putting my hands in front of my eyes. The kids thought it was great, and were enjoying the breathtaking view. We stopped at a spectacular place, where it was a little wider and Toby took my picture sitting by the edge of the road. After taking it, I looked over the side of the road and CRAWLED back to the car. It was almost straight down (about a mile). We got back in the car and continued up. We rounded a corner and my hands went over my eyes again, and I said "Oh No!" We were on top of the ridge, with nothing on either side. It was so narrow, that you could not step out of the car on either side without falling over the edge, but what a view! It was like being in an open airplane. Well, we drove on, and all at once we turned on to a good paved road. We had made a wrong turn somewhere and had been on a road that wasn't even on the map. "Never a dull moment!!!"

We left one morning for a trip to Las Canadas, which was at the foot of the highest mountain in Spain, Teide. We drove first through lush valleys that soon changed to a surprising Alpine landscape with tall, though very different looking pine trees. We stopped at many scenic places to take pictures and just to look and admire the beautiful scenery and view. As we drove on, everything changed again, as we were now in a rugged mountain area with volcanic rocks and craters and strange looking plants. It looked as if we had just arrived on another planet. In fact, we saw a spaceship amongst the rocks which had been used for a science fiction movie that was filmed there. There was one mountain in particular where the lava had run halfway down before it cooled and hardened.

By now, the time was about 2 o clock and everybody was starving. We finally arrived at the Parador half an hour later. I want to explain here about the Parador; it is a government-run hotel and restaurant for the tourists, always located at the most beautiful spots anywhere in Spain. This one was located directly at the foot of Teide, inside the world's largest crater. There we had I think one of the biggest dinners ever. The first course consisted of nine to ten different types of hors deuvers, and soup. For the second course, I had fish, the kids had spaghetti, and Toby had eggs with tomatoes. For the third and main course, Toby and I had veal cutlets with potatoes and vegetables and the kids had giant portions of chicken, potatoes and vegetables. We barely made it through dessert for which the kids had mantecado (ice cream) and we had "Torte Parador." The price for all of this came to about two dollars per person. After dinner, we walked around a little (we really needed that) and then started on our trip home. About halfway down, the kids were quite excited because the clouds, being lower than we were, were coming straight at us. They really thought that was great and Susie started to sing, "Catch a falling cloud and put it in your pocket, save it for a sunny day." However the clouds were very thick and we "grownups" were glad to get out of it because it was dangerous driving.

When driving around the island, you can tell just about what altitude you are at by the plant life. You start off at sea level with banana trees and poinsettias, and then as you go up, there is a wide belt of cactus plants (all kinds), poppies, geraniums, and "dragon trees." Next come the pine trees, a kind that grows only here, with the biggest pine cones we had ever seen, then a huge tumbleweed type of thing, and then nothing but lava, of all types and colors, and still higher you run into snow. Which reminds me: One day we had planned a trip around the island, but everything seemed to go against us. In the morning, it looked real cloudy and Toby said we would probably be better off going south along the coast. But I, remembering the bad road and truck traffic, talked him out of it and we went via the mountain. At the foot of the mountain, the sun was shining, but the higher we went, the worse it got, with clouds and fog. Finally, we reached a point where there was snow. We stopped to consider if we should turn back or go on, but since the sun had started to peek through the clouds, we decided to go on. After a few curves, the snow was deeper and we met a car coming down. It was a Spaniard and his Senora. He stopped his car, came out and told us it was "impossible" to go on any farther. Then he reached in his car and took out a large knife.... .a huge sausage and a bottle of champagne. We all had something of it. The champagne was delicious and "was supposed to warm us up," he said. We then gave them some of our cheese sandwiches and had a great time. Just about then, a German couple in a camper van pulled up behind us, more talk and champagne, more fun—then a taxi and two more cars. Out came another bottle of champagne, more fun. Well, after all the goodies were gone, we helped each other turn around, which wasn't easy on that narrow road. We shook hands all the way around and said goodbye, and headed down with another pleasant experience under our belts.

We made quite a few friends on Tenerife. There was one neighbor who was a retired Swedish dentist; another was Senora Timmermann, a German lady, who gave us some much-needed Spanish lessons, and then there were some Spanish neighbors and their children. Susie and Gary were playing with the neighbor kids and were picking up some Spanish. We sometimes sent them to buy groceries for us, but we didn't always get what we wanted. One time we sent Gary to buy a cucumber. We looked up the word for it in the English-Spanish dictionary, but he came home with something green, that looked like a giant cucumber, but it wasn't. We never could figure out what it was. When Toby and I went grocery-shopping, we couldn't always quite get across what we wanted, the saleswoman would then take me by the hand and bring me behind the counter and tell me to pick out what I needed. There were no big supermarkets at that time; most of the stores were small and run by their owners. Many times there would be several customers in front of me, and I would tell them that it wasn't my turn, but the other ladies would just smile and say they didn't mind. It wasn't every day that Americans would shop at their store.

We found out there was a German school in Santa Cruz and since I had dual citizenship, the Herr Director had to take our kids. He didn't really want to, since our kids only spoke English, and the school was taught in German and Spanish. He finally agreed to take Karin (thirteen), Kenny (twelve) and Susie (nine) as guests. Karin thought we sent her to the German school because we hated her, but we really wanted, especially Karin, to meet some kids her own age. Of course, it was hard for them, not knowing the language. To everybody's surprise, the kids liked it in school, especially the girls. Susie told us that every morning the class got up when the teacher came in and said: "Guten Morgen Herr ..." then right afterwards they said "Buenos Dias Senor ..." but after Susie got there, they added a third greeting "Good morning Susie." She had so much fun. The language barrier didn't bother her at all.

We were quite a novelty there, not so much because we were Americans, but because of our four kids. (And they behaved amazingly well in public.) Another crowd attractor was our car. There were all kinds of cars there, from Rolls Royces to Cadillacs and Volkswagens, but not another Dodge van. People stopped and admired it wherever we went. When we passed slowly through towns, we heard "bonito coche" (good looking car).

In the beginning of February, we took a boat over to the next island, Gran Canaria. We arrived at about 12 PM, siesta time, and we were told we couldn't have our van unloaded until 2 PM. So we took a taxi to a nearby restaurant to have lunch. It was a real nice place; we were sitting outside and they had music playing over the loudspeaker. At 1:30, Toby told Karin, Susie, Gary and me, "Why don't you stay here and Kenny and I will get the van at the dock." Well, we waited and waited; we could hear at least three sets of repeating music over the loudspeaker, and still no Toby or Kenny. I had no money with me and couldn't pay. The waiter kept on asking if we wanted anything else. I finally made him understand that I was waiting for my husband to come back. At last, it must have been more than two hours later, they came back. Toby was so mad, they just didn't get around to unloading our van until about 4 o clock.

We spent the first two days looking for a house to rent and finally found a four-bedroom villa in a beautiful valley. The kids wanted it right away. Because of the view; no, because it had a big game room with ping pong table and an electric football game outfit. They wouldn't have cared less where the house was located.

At first we didn't like this island too much, but it turned out to be quite interesting, in a different way than the first one and the beaches were much bigger and better. Toby tried to drive all the way around the island one day but as the road got real bad, we met a taxi full of English tourists who had come from the way we wanted to go. They stopped and told us that the road got worse and that they had been terrified. Even the cab driver said it had taken him an hour and a half to drive thirty miles. They already had started to leave, when one woman leaned out of the window and warned us again, "Don't go, you cawn't do that to the children … "So we turned around and headed back and all the way back home the kids were saying in their best English accents "You cawn't do that to the children."

On another day, we found the caves of the Guanches. These primitive people used the caves as dwellings a long time ago. There was a steep walk going up to the honeycomb shaped caves. The kids had a great time crawling in and out of the little tunnels and sitting in the "honeycombs." It made me a little nervous at times to see them disappear and then pop up again. It was a child's dream, a perfect place to play hide and seek. All this climbing up and down made us very warm and we thought it was time to look for a nice beach, which we found. It was the perfect ending for a perfect day.

Although the weather didn't look very promising, we left one afternoon on our trip to Tamadaba. The farther we got up into the mountains, the worse the weather was, until we finally didn't see the view at all anymore, only just enough of the road ahead for driving. I told Toby that we absolutely should turn back, but of course he insisted that he KNEW it was going to clear up in just a little while, and to my amazement (and I think his too) it really did. We didn't see too much in Tamadaba, but we found a nice place to stop where the kids could climb down to a waterfall, pick flowers and collect pine cones. On the way back it had cleared completely, so we could see all the scenery we missed in the fog. We also had bypassed a huge crater, one of the scenic wonders of the island. We almost missed it again, but we stopped, since it was marked as a picture spot. Only after a drive up a little hill could one see that giant red and black crater. We decided from now on to stop at every picture spot, with the next one coming up shortly thereafter. Again it didn't look like anything. We parked the car and asked a young boy if this was the mirador (picture spot). He showed us through a gateway which led through a mountain. On the other side was a restaurant with part of the mountain used for walls, real interesting and what a view!! We could see a whole chain of mountains and valleys and also some cave homes built right into the mountains.

Every morning, the whole time we lived in the house in Las Palmas, a bread man came to the door and we bought fresh bread from him. Toby always dealt with him and when Toby asked the man how much he owed, the man would reply so fast, so that Toby never understood him. So he just held out some money on his hand and let him take whatever was needed. This went on almost every day until the day we left. Toby had finally figured out what he was saying and gave him the exact change. The man's face lit up and he said "Bueno Senor." Of course Toby then tipped him very well.

On March 6, we left Gran Canaria and took a boat over to the island of Lanzarote. What a night it was! The boat was rocking all night long. This had to have been the worst boat ride so far, even worse than crossing the Atlantic. We arrived the next day in Arrecife, Lanzarote. We had made reservations at the Parador and knew exactly where to go. We had a whole suite there, with two bedrooms and a bathroom, very nice. This turned out to be Toby's favorite island, very few tourists, the people quite unspoiled and the scenery, as he said," fantastic"

Once again the weather didn't look too promising, but we started out the next day for our northern trip anyway. The roads were very badly marked and you really didn't know if you were going where you wanted to go. Soon it started to rain and we couldn't see very much. To our surprise we came out at our destination, the Miromar el Rio, a lookout point from where you were supposed to see the isle of Graciosa. But all we could see was a few yards of road ahead of us. I urged Toby to turn around, but as usual, he insisted on going on. We stopped for a while and Toby and the kids started collecting pretty looking snails. Since I was afraid to go on in this kind of weather, I urged them to find some more snails, hoping that in the meantime the clouds would pass over. Sure enough, it really went according to plan, and we did get to see the island, with its white sand, a real beautiful view. As we drove on (with an ashtray full of very smelly live snails), we were really on a "cliff hanger" as Toby called it. Boy was I glad it had cleared up. We drove back another way and were now looking for the "green caves." After a few wrong turns and asking many natives for directions, we finally found the right road. On the way, we stopped at a rocky beach that was covered with beautiful sea shells. There was only one thing wrong. By now the rain was pouring down, but that didn't stop the real beachcombers! After a while, we were all soaked. We were just about ready to leave when the rain finally stopped. Of course, that was reason enough to stay a while longer, and it was good that we did, because the wind dried us all up again. We also stopped somewhere in what seemed to be no-man's land and bought a bunch of bananas, five kilos to be exact (about eleven pounds), and ate them all up to the last one.

We finally got to the green caves, after almost passing by them. There were two openings. We went into one by way of a little path. We walked until we couldn't see any more and were just about ready to leave when a man came out of nowhere and asked us if we wanted to see the caves. There was a fee of 40 cents per person. However, we only had to get two tickets, with the children going for free. Now the real tour began. The lights were turned on, with eerie music playing and the guide took us through the spectacular caves with all kinds of rocks, from crystal to sandstone in all colors. What impressed me the most was where the melted stone had dropped down, forming "icicles" all over the ceiling of the caves. At one point, the guide cautioned us about a very deep cliff. He took us to the edge from where we carefully looked over. He then picked up a stone, gave it to Kenny and told him to throw it down over the edge of the cliff, which he did. We all expected to wait a while for the rock to hit bottom. To everybody's surprise, we only heard a small splash and found out it was not a hole in the ground at all, but only the reflection of the roof of the cave in only a few inches of the clearest water. This was a real hit with the kids; they thought that was really something. The caves were seven kilometers long; we went through about 1 kilometer. They were still working on the rest. At another point, just about at the end of the cave, there was a rock formation that looked like an arrow that was pointing to the exit of the cave. There was also a monster face up on the ceiling, grinning fiendishly at us. We came out to the right of the entrance, which we first thought was another cave. On the way back to the Parador we stopped in town and booked a tour for the next day to see the fire mountain.

At 10 AM, a bus picked us up at the Parador for our tour. We were a real international group with a Spaniard for the driver, an English woman, a young Swedish boy, a couple from Belgium and we German-Danish-Americans. We headed south through farmlands where tomatoes, onions, corn and more was grown under the worst conditions we had ever seen, and yet quite successfully. We admired the way the farmers grew the grapes in little pockets with neatly stacked lava stones as borders for protection from the wind. There was a lot of wind on this island. These little pockets were built and planted all the way up and around the mountain.

We then drove on to Playa Blanca, home to a large salt plant where salt was extracted from the ocean through a slow evaporation process. Next we went on to El Golfo, a green lagoon, located right next to the blue ocean. What made the lagoon bright green was that the entire bottom was covered with green rock crystals. The cliffs above it were wild too, red and orange. On the way to this place, we drove through two giant lava beds which once were two rivers of lava coming from the mountain of fire, flowing all the way to the ocean.

After our picnic lunch, we drove to the fire mountain. Although this volcano wasn't active at that time, it was still quite hot. When you dug a little in the sand with your hands, you could feel the hot earth. Somebody had brought along some eggs, they buried them in the hot sand, and soon after, dug out hard boiled eggs. A boy threw a dried tumble weed into a hole, and it immediately burst into flames. He also poured a pail of water into the hole, which came right back up like a huge geyser, all this for our entertainment.

The bus driver then took us to the other side of the mountain where our four camels were waiting for us. Karin and Kenny, with Susie on top had one, the other passengers of the tour had two more and Toby and I with Gary on top had the orneriest one of the bunch. He was complaining right from the start. The getting up and sitting down of the camel is quite an experience in itself. It was fun riding the camels up the hill; only the wind was blowing real hard and cold. Our camel didn't like it at all and he showed it. The kids really had a great time. Their camel tender would stop their camel for a while and then catch up with the rest by making the camel go faster. However our man didn't like it, because it made our camel ornerier. After all that, it was time for our trip back to Arrecife. This sure was an adventure for all of us.

Two days before our ship to mainland Spain was due in Las Palmas, we headed back to Gran Canaria and stayed a couple of days at the Parador up in the mountains. We had mixed feelings about leaving the islands, glad and sad. Most of the people were very nice and the climate and scenery were terrific, but there were some drawbacks. There was the slight undercurrent of a police state. (Not as bad as mainland Spain though). Franco had a very strong reign on his people. Two letters we wrote to Toby's sister were opened and sealed with scotch tape. It had stamped on them in Spanish "permitted to enter the United States." I'm sure many of our postcards never "got off the ground." Yet they treated foreigners very well and wanted foreign investments.

The ship to Spain was packed with people and cars. Our van was up on deck, which was quite handy. Since we could only get third class passage on the ship, the cabins were very small. We spent most of the trip sitting in the van, with everybody grinning and asking us how we are enjoying our "drive to Spain."

We got off the boat at Malaga and drove up to Granada, where we spent the night. The Spanish countryside was really nice, neat as a pin, but no place was as beautiful as the area around Granada, with the Sierra Nevada Mountains and the rich, lush valleys in spring time bloom.

The next morning we drove up through Madrid to Zaragoza. We were lost in Madrid for 1 1/2 hours because of road construction detours. We stopped one time to try and get our bearings, but a local policeman, complete with machine gun, told us to move on. We asked him to tell us the way out to Barcelona, but he just told us to move. I argued with him, while Toby was looking at the map. Well, a crowd of nervous people gathered very quickly and a man came over and told Toby in broken English that we had better go "while we could," so we did. We drove a few more blocks and we found another place to stop. While we were looking at our map, a city bus stopped to let off a passenger. The bus driver then got out and asked if we were lost, we said yes, and that we wanted to go to Barcelona. We must have looked real down, because he said "follow me." Then he and his passengers led us to "Avaneda de Barcelona." When we parted all the people on the bus waved goodbye to us. All during our time on the islands and in Spain, the Spaniards really impressed us as a genuinely nice, friendly and helpful people.

When we got to Barcelona, we were shocked by the amount of smog there. We didn't get to see very much of the town because of this. The following day we decided to drive right through to Augsburg, Germany, my hometown.

We drove along the coast of the Mediterranean and stopped occasionally to admire the view. It was getting on toward evening when we crossed the French border. Much to our surprise, all the car headlights were orange. We were a little concerned about that and worried that we would get stopped by the police and lose time. So we stopped at the first grocery store and looked for something wrapped in clear orange tinted cellophane. At last we found a large bag of walnuts packaged with the "right stuff." Toby taped the wrapper on the headlights and it worked just fine. We crossed into Switzerland a few hours later. We were all quite tired and decided to catch a little sleep in the van in a shopping center parking lot in Geneva. We awoke very early and went to a gas station, and while Toby was filling up the car and checking it, the kids and I were inside getting us breakfast from the many vending machines that were there. We then headed north through Bern and a few hours later crossed the Rhine river at Schaffhausen into Germany. What we saw of Switzerland was very spectacular (and the roads were great). Later that afternoon (it was just before Easter); we arrived at my mother's house to a warm welcome and a great meal. The next day, all the German relatives that Karin and Kenny had never met, came to visit. I remember the kids saying that they just closed their minds when everybody was talking German, since they didn't understand anything.

We did a lot of sight seeing in my hometown of Augsburg, which is now over 2000 years old. It was first established in the year 15 BC by the Romans. Part of the original town wall is still there, as well as lots of Roman artifacts from the time of Claudius. The Augsburger Dom (cathedral) had the very first stained glass windows in the world. Some of them were destroyed during the air raid, but most of them remained intact. You could see paintings by Hans Holbein there. Augsburg also has the very first social village inside the city. It was built in 1516 by one of the richest people of that time, the Fugger family. To this day, needy retired people can live in very comfortable apartments for 1 Euro a year and a prayer, but they have to be born in Augsburg and have lived there all their lives. My hometown is also called the third "Mozart Town" after Salzburg and Vienna. Mozart's father was born in Augsburg and Wolfgang came to Augsburg quite often to visit his relatives. We even have a Mozart Haus there.

In April, we drove up to Denmark to visit Toby's relatives. Toby had two half sisters and lots of uncles, aunts and cousins in the Copenhagen area. We arrived just in time for Hjordis (Toby's sister) and Harald's 25th wedding anniversary. We stayed a couple of days with Hjordis and then Toby's uncle Daniel found us a little cottage by the Baltic Sea with very primitive facilities. However, we were on our own and could visit relatives at our leisure. I know now what if feels like when everybody is talking and you don't understand anything. Although most of the Danish relatives spoke English very well, they would start out speaking English, but would soon go back to Danish again.

We visited all the interesting places like Rosenburg Castle, Halmlet's Castle and Tivoli (a Danish type Disneyland); this was of course the kids' favorite. One of Toby's cousins owned a pig farm, and the kids got such a kick out of it when he told them that they were invited to come to his "funny farm." It took quite a while to explain to the Danes what "funny farm" means in American slang.

On Mothers day, the kids picked tulips for me in a big field. We were on our way to dinner at one of the aunt's houses. Aunt Inger took the tulips and thought we had brought them for her. We didn't know that this was the custom when you are invited to dinner. The kids weren't going to have that, and wanted me to have those flowers. We finally got it all straightened out.

One time we were invited for dinner at Toby's other half sister's apartment. Irene had a maid who cooked and served the dinner. Our kids were very impressed; they had never been served by a maid before.

We spent about two weeks in Denmark and had a very good time there. We also made a side trip to Malmö, Sweden, which was also very interesting. After we came back to Augsburg, we took quite a few trips around Bavaria and Austria and also drove through Liechtenstein.

One time we took my mother, my sister Gerda, her husband Sepp, and my niece Sonja on a trip to Rothenburg in our van. We all had a great time. It was funny to see Sonja not quite knowing what to make of all her American cousins. She was ten years old and up to now she had been the only grandchild of her Oma, but now she had to share the attention with four more of Oma's grandchildren. However, being an only child she soon was happy to have her four cousins around.

After a few weeks, it was time for us to settle down and for Toby to look for a job. We were now living in the same apartment that I grew up in; the only thing different about it was that my mother now had a shower in her bathroom. My mother let us have two rooms and of course the run of the whole apartment.

Relatives donated furniture to us and that makes me think of something really funny that happened. Gerda's mother-in-law gave us a large armoire (in Germany there are no built-in closets; you store your clothes in an armoire). She lived on the second floor and it was quite hard to carry the armoire down the stairs. Sepp and his brother-in-law Hans were in front and Toby in the back as they carried it down the stairs. Sepp and Hans kept on saying in German "ab," which sounds exactly like "up" in English. However,"ab" in German means "down." So they kept on telling Toby "ab" and Toby kept on lifting the armoire up, he lifted it farther and farther up, almost up over their heads. Finally I came along and told Toby that they were not saying up, they were saying ab, which meant down. Toby said afterwards he thought he was going to get a hernia if he kept that UP any longer.

Our kids adjusted to German life quite easily. They made friends with German children and Karin found a good friend in Lucia, an Italian girl that lived in the same apartment building. We were joking about her learning German with an Italian accent.

We also enrolled the kids in the Kapellenschule, the same school I attended as a child. By now they were doing a little better with their German. One of the things they did in German schools (in my time and at the time our kids were there) was this: When they had recess, all the kids were required to walk around in a circle in the hallway (during bad weather). Each class had their own space for that. Well, it would never have occurred to me to question WHY we had to do that; you just did what your teacher told you, period. However, in come our American kids and they thought that was the silliest thing to do and just didn't want any part of that. Of course, the teachers told them to walk like the rest of the children and our kids asked the teachers why they had to do such a silly thing as going around in circles. The teachers were stunned. Nobody had ever asked before and I think they momentarily didn't really know themselves; it just never came up. Well, later on the teachers told the class the reason they were told to walk around was because after a long time of sitting still, it was good for them to have some exercise. That made sense to our kids and from then on, they walked around in circles with the rest of them.

We had Gary enrolled in the first grade and it was the custom for every child to receive a big cone-shaped bag, filled with candy. All the German parents gave them to their first graders to take with them to the first day of school. Gary was quite pleased with that. Of course, our other kids said that that was not fair; they never got any big bag of candy on their first day of school.

Things sure were different for all of us, living in such close quarters. We always had a house of our own with a big yard, and now all we had was a two-room apartment. The kids took on some of the habits of the Germans. For instance, in the beginning they made fun of the people looking out the windows for entertainment. But it didn't take long for them to get a pillow for the window sill, so they could comfortably hang out the window to see what was going on down on the street. One thing they got a kick out of was that every once in while a farmer came with a horse and a wagon down the street, rang the bell of all the apartment dwellers and yelled up the hallway, "Kartoffel" (potatoes). People bought potatoes in big quantities, and buying directly from the farmer was a good deal.

The only one who couldn't get used to this kind of life was Toby. He was constantly pacing the floor out of boredom. He always had things to do at home and here was absolutely nothing for him to do. He had no luck finding a job. All the American government jobs were no longer available, because the civilian employees who had been living and working in France now took all the jobs in Germany. While we were up in Denmark, his Aunt Olga gave him the complete works of Shakespeare and that's what he read while living in the apartment. Since the kids were in school now, we couldn't travel around as much any more.

By summer 1967, we realized that Toby wasn't going to find a job in Europe. We talked it over and decided that if he didn't find anything by September, we would go back home to the United States. At this time, we also enrolled our kids in summer school for American dependents of the Army. We didn't have to pay anything at the German school in Tenerife or Augsburg, but we were required to pay 100 dollars to enroll them into the American school. They didn't have anything for Gary our first grader, so only Karin, Kenny, and Susie attended the school at the American base. In summer school, they repeated what was being taught for the past year. Since our kids attended school only for a short time on and off for the whole year, this turned out to be a good way for them to be prepared for the next school year in America.

As fall approached (and our money ran low), we decided it was time to head back home. We talked it over and since we were from Michigan, we decided to go back by way of Canada rather than New York. We found a Russian luxury liner that would leave from Bremerhaven, Germany, stop in England, and then sail on to Montreal, Canada, not far from Detroit, Michigan. It was 1967, and it would be quite an adventure to learn more about Russian people. So we booked passage for ourselves and our van in October. We said our sad goodbyes to family and friends (and our footloose and fancy-free life style) and headed for the port. When we got to the ship, we found that the van had to be sterilized (steam cleaned) before they loaded it. Once we had that done, we boarded the ship. It was called the "Alexander Pushkin" (named after a famous Russian writer of the early 1900s), a really splendid ship, 577 feet long and 79 feet wide with nine decks. Our first contact with the Russians was with the stern-faced people who checked our passports. Then an equally glum steward showed us to our cabins. The kids came into our cabin when he left; we all felt that we had made a big mistake in taking this ship and that it was going to be a pretty grim trip. The cabins were nice and comfortable and we all got a kick out of seeing "hot and cold" on the faucets, in Russian.

The next morning, we went to breakfast and were amazed at the quality and quantity of food and fruit on a long table by the entrance of the dining room. The table was loaded down like this for every meal. We were also happy to find that the waiters and waitresses and room stewards were actually pleasant people and that most, if not all, spoke English. There was also a nice area for the kids to go to, with planned activities and games, which they really liked. It had to be well done, because the kids on board were from all over the world.

We didn't really expect a Russian ship to have luxuries as we "capitalists" understood them, but it did. It had two swimming pools, a gymnasium, library, five bars, shops, lounges, barber and beauty shops, a movie theater, air conditioning, play rooms for the kids, three elevators, outdoor and indoor dance floors, and medical facilities with an operating room. We were surprised and impressed.

When we stopped in England, we were told we would have a day to spend there. We started out on a train and then transferred to the subway, which took us to the city of London. Then we took a bus tour of the city, which included all the important sights of London, for example Buckingham Palace, the Tower of

London, the Tower Bridge, and Westminster Cathedral. After the tour, we went down to the subway to return to the ship, and while we were waiting for the train we met a nice Englishman who shared some apples with our kids.

One evening the ship had an amateur talent night for the passengers, which was mostly corny, but fun. Even our kids dressed up, Karin as a horse jockey, and Kenny in an Arabic costume. When somebody asked Kenny why he dressed up as an Arab, he was told that the kids had in fact been to Morocco not long ago.

Then a few nights later it was the crew's turn to entertain us. Well, we were amazed again, as the crew put on an excellent show. We found out later that many professional entertainers were picked as crew members, because the Russian luxury ships were "showcases" to the outside world. The crew/entertainers were also very happy with the set-up, because they could travel, and had some freedom.

There was a die-hard communist man who kept trying to draw Toby into political conversations whenever he saw him alone, but after talking to Toby he gave up on him as a "lost cause" very quickly.

There was a lot to do on the ship, and the time went by quickly. Soon we were sailing down the St. Lawrence River and docking in Montreal. We said our good-byes to the people we had met and to the crew members we had contact with. One nice thing about Communist employees (at that time) was that they couldn't accept tips (that's capitalistic). But we gave them each a souvenir that they did accept: a Kennedy half dollar. They had a lot of respect for him.

We then left the ship and when our van was unloaded, we piled in and took off. The van was now very crowded with all our stuff, so the first thing we did was rent a U-haul trailer in Montreal, so we could all be comfortable. It was a long drive to the U.S./Canadian border, and we were all very tired when we got there.

We weren't looking forward to going through customs. We didn't really have anything to declare, but of course they didn't know that, and could make us unload everything. When we came to the border we woke up the kids so they could experience "going across" to the good old U.S.A. The U.S. custom official said, "Hi, been doing a little camping?" Toby said "Yes" and he waved us through. Needless to say, we were very happy to be back in the U.S.A.

To this day, the kids say that the trip was a fantastic experience that they will always remember and, of course, we agree.

Ready for adventure

The Casbah in Tangier, Morocco

On the edge, on Tenerife Island

International picnic

The curvy roads on Grand Canary Island

Karin, Susie, Gary and Kenny with "Camel Driver" on Lanzarote Island

In Rothenburg, Germany

All the Danish cousins at the "Funny Farm" in Denmark

At the palace in Copenhagen, Denmark   Gary's first day of school in Augsburg

In the Alps in Liechtenstein

BACK IN THE GOOD OLD U.S.A.

My German friend, Barbara, found a house for us to rent in Grand Ledge, Michigan. So we had a place to go to right away. It was a real old house with lots of things wrong with it, but we had a place to stay. The old lady who used to live there had just died and her nephew rented the house to us. It came with all the furniture and everything there was for sale. We bought a few things to get started again; one was a beautiful carved old chair, and I think I paid fifteen dollars for it.

Our kids were all able to advance to the next grade, as though they had never left. The school always wanted me to give some information as to where they went to school in Europe, but we kept telling them that the paper-work was on the way and soon they forgot about it, since our kids had no problem fitting back in with the rest of the kids.

Shortly after we returned from our trip, Toby got his old job back again, so we sold our van and started looking for a house in Grand Ledge. When Christmas 1967 came around Toby asked me what I would like to have for a present. I told him I would like an unusual plant. We celebrate Christmas on Christmas Eve and the kids usually can't hardly wait to open their presents. However, that year was different. All the excitement was about MY present. They told me to leave the room because they had to prepare my surprise. Finally I was allowed in the living room and there it was, my "unusual plant," a bare branch in a vase, and on it were 100 brand new one dollar bills. I really was stunned as I didn't think there was any extra money available. Only then did the kids look for their own presents. The story is not complete because I left the branch in the sand and water because I could see some green buds on it. Shortly after, in the middle of the winter, there were actually lilac blossoms on that branch, lilacs being my favorite flower.

We finally found, and bought a house in Grand Ledge. We used the money from the sale of the van as a down payment. The house was almost 100 years old and looked like an old two-story farmhouse. We paid 18,500 dollars for it. The house was located in town with the back yard backing up to the Grand River.

When we came back to Grand Ledge, all of our four kids advanced to their respective classes. Although their schooling, during the eleven months that we were overseas, was not exactly regular, their experience in living abroad was very educational.

Shortly after they started school, I was approached by the Spanish teacher in Karin's class who asked me to show some of the slides from our trip. It started with just one class, but soon the geography class and many others wanted to see the slides also, so they decided to have the slide show at the high school auditorium, with many classes present. It was very interesting for me to see our pictures on a movie-size screen. Karin was a little embarrassed at first, but since all her friends seemed to like it, she was OK with it.

I also showed the slides in Gary's second grade class and the kids all wrote me thank you letters, which I have to this day. One letter I really liked said, "Thank you Mrs. Torngren I really liked your show, especially because it got us out of going to class." The children's favorite picture was the one where the clouds were below us.

Soon after we moved into our house, our next door neighbor, an elderly widow, came over to welcome us to the neighborhood. All of a sudden, she said very accusingly, "where did you get that chair? This was my mother's chair". I told her that I bought it from the man that rented a house to us. It turned out that he was her nephew. She was quite upset, but she wasn't going to get that chair from me. Besides, she already had a whole house full of antiques (I still have that chair to this day).

Since we were close to the river, there were always a lot of bats flying around in the evening. One night we woke up because we heard a noise. We turned on the light and saw a bat flying around in our bedroom. Toby pulled off his sheet, put it around his shoulders, got his tennis racket out of the closet and went bat hunting. He got no help from me; I stayed under the covers, laughing hysterically. When he saw the bat way up high on the wall directly across from the window, he went outside in his sheet-outfit with a pellet gun. He was going to shoot him through the open window. But by that time the bat was gone. Imagine seeing a guy with a sheet around him, trying to shoot into the window. I sure was glad nobody saw him. After all that excitement, we went back to sleep. In the morning, Toby took the shirt he was going to wear to work from the closet, and there was the bat, hanging upside down on the pocket of his shirt. He wrapped the shirt around the bat and carried him outside. End of bat story!! Toby did some extensive remodeling of the house and added two bedrooms in the attic.

One day Karin and I decided to take a ceramic class together. The class was located in a couple's home right there in Grand Ledge. Karin made a beer stein for her Dad and I made a pretty bowl. To get started, you had to select the greenware, which was located in their basement. They had wooden shelves from top to bottom, with greenware on all the shelves. Some of the shelves were bending with the weight of it. Karin and I were alone in the basement choosing what we were going to make next. I selected one item from the shelf, honest to goodness, that's all I did, when the whole shelf unit collapsed with all the greenware broken on the floor. Upstairs they heard the crash and the owners came running down. I started crying, wondering what it would cost me to replace everything. Well they decided all I had to pay was fifteen dollars, what a relief! Karin, who was about fifteen years old at the time, was very embarrassed. After we paid the fifteen dollars, we left immediately, never to return.

Around this time we bought forty acres in the little town of Saranac, which is located between Grand Rapids and Ionia. We thought that some day we would build a house there and maybe subdivide it. We paid 8,500 dollars for it. The former owner of the land paid us for letting him graze his cows there. On weekends we would drive there in our Oldsmobile Toronado, a very big car. We would drive right through the meadow which actually was quite hilly. It was a wonder we did not ruin the car. Sometimes the cows would come up to the car and lick it. What fun! Also I might mention that on the property next door was a nudist camp.

Late 1970, actually just before Christmas, Toby lost his job in Ionia, because the company was sold. One day a real estate agent (the same one that sold us the house) came to our door to ask if we wanted to sell our house. He was showing a house across the street and the people pointed at our house and said that is what they were looking for. It didn't take us long to decide to sell the house. We asked 24,000 dollars for it and got it. We then rented an old farmhouse outside of Lansing. As part of the rent Toby renovated the upstairs.

Toby not only worked on houses, he also fixed up cars. One such car was a Rambler station wagon he found in a wrecking yard. It had heavy front-end body damage, but very low mileage and was otherwise in very good condition. He then bought a 65 Rambler parts car with a bad engine. After taking off all the necessary repair parts, the parts car had to be taken to the dump. You could still do that at that time for a very small sum of money, about ten dollars. The plan was for Toby to tow the parts car to the dump, with me steering the car. I was not too happy about this arrangement, but we took off. What Toby didn't know was that the parts car started pumping oil all over my windshield. I couldn't see anything!!

I also couldn't let him know of my problem since the horn wasn't working. I was crying all the way to the dump. When we got there I was very shook up, but then we untied the parts car and pushed it over the embankment. The trials and tribulations of Maya!!

I was still meeting with the Overseas Wives Club in Lansing. We got a new member; her name was Rosina. Her husband had just been transferred from San Francisco to manage a hotel in Lansing. She kept telling me how great California was and that she couldn't wait to get back again. On a real cold and wet winter day in March, I told Toby all about what Rosina had said to me about California. Toby had been stationed in California in 1946 and had been very impressed with the area. So we talked about it and decided since he was out of work here, with not much hope of finding anything soon, we might as well live somewhere where the weather is nice, and he could look for work there. Toby then took Kenny along in a 67 Toronado which he had repaired, and drove out to California to look things over. They had to go the southern route since there was still a lot of snow farther north. He knew some people at Mack Trucks in Hayward, California, and had been offered a job just before our trip, but they weren't hiring at the time, however, they said that there might be something for him later. When Toby and Kenny came back, we really started planning our move. Toby fixed up another car, a long Dodge van, which we would drive to California. After school was out in June, Toby and Gary made a final trip to California in the restored Rambler station wagon and rented a house for us in Fremont, California.

Outstanding

Sept. 23, 1970

Our Trip

We left at a port in New York.
The ship floats like a cork.
We had a long journey across the ocean,
We all got seasick from the motion.
We saw Canary Islands 1-2-3.
And picked bananas from the tree.
We went to Marrocco and then to Spain.
There was lots of sunshine and no rain.
We went to France and Switzerland,
We saw lots of things we thoght were grand.
Then went to Denmark, Germany.
And my Grandmother was waiting for me.

By Gary Forngren

Gary's poem about the trip

Maya and her "unusual plant"

CALIFORNIA HERE WE COME

In July, the time had finally arrived and we were ready to roll. Karin had decided that she wouldn't be coming with us. She just graduated from high school and she was planning to attend college in Michigan. She was going to stay with her friend Becky's family until school started. It was very hard for us to leave her behind. Susie had made a big sign that said "California here we come" and fastened it on to the side window of the van. We were loaded (overloaded) with all our belongings inside and on the roof rack of the van and also in a rented trailer. We were so weighted down that we could only drive forty to fifty miles per hour. When we got to Iowa, Toby stopped the car at a gas station and gave me an ultimatum: Either we get a moving truck, which I was supposed to drive, or he was going to go to the dump and get rid of everything on top of the van and in the trailer. I never was a willing long distance driver, but what choice did I have? Of course, we rented a truck, took most of the stuff off the top of the van and got rid of the trailer. I drove the truck all the way to California. Toby had taken pictures of California on his previous trips, but as we were approaching California I was very disappointed with the scenery in Nevada. However, as soon as we crossed the border, California showed itself in all its splendor. We arrived in Fremont and I fell in love with the Bay area right away.

As it was just shortly before the 4th of July, we saw fireworks booths everywhere. In Michigan, the sale of any fireworks was illegal. Kenny and Gary and Toby too, could hardly wait to buy some of that stuff, and from then on "the boys" always had lots of fun on the 4th of July.

Toby went to the unemployment office, but could not find any jobs. We were getting very low on money; as a matter of fact, all we had left was 100 dollars. When Toby told this to the woman there and also that he had three dependent children, she said that he should apply for welfare. Toby however could not do this; he was too proud and told her he would wait for one more week. When he came back home, I told him there was a phone call from Mack Trucks and that they were offering him a job and he could start the next day. What a relief!!!

Shortly after we arrived in California, we decided to take a drive down the coast on scenic highway 1 to Big Sur. The view was so beautiful and we stopped at several places. At one of the places, we could see some big boulders that looked like jade and Toby and the kids, Kenny, Susie and Gary thought there might be smaller pieces to collect. They were all rock hunters. Anyway, they all climbed down the very steep bank to the Pacific and sure enough, there were lots of pieces of jade. On the way up they grabbed some of the bushes and Toby was stabbed by one of the branches. We came from Michigan and knew what poison ivy looked like, but none of us knew what poison oak was like. They all very soon found out. We went to a motel in Morrow Bay and they all took a shower right away, but it was too late. The next morning, all of them showed severe poison oak symptoms. The worst off was Susie and Toby. Susie's face was so swollen that she was unrecognizable. Toby had an infection in his leg that looked so bad, we had to go to Emergency. Gary got infected a little bit and Kenny was lucky not to get it at all. So ended our very first vacation in California. From then on we respected Poison Oak. Whenever our relatives from Europe were visiting us, we really scared them and told them to be careful. (Poison oak and ivy is not native to Europe).

By late fall, we were looking for a house to buy. We told our real estate agent that we first had to sell our forty acres in Michigan. I think when he heard that, he thought we must have a lot of money, but he soon found out otherwise when we finally sold our property for 10,500 dollars, a far cry from California properties. We now had our down payment for a house in Fremont. We moved in just before Christmas 1971. Christmas Eve we experienced our very first earthquake. It was interesting seeing the Christmas tree walking across the floor.

The house was an older ranch-style house, for which we paid $26,000. The best part was the view. We could see all the way to the other side of the bay. At night, it was a wonderful sight with all the lights. The living room had a long narrow window. Toby replaced it immediately with a large glass door and installed a deck. We could now really enjoy the view. We never got tired of it. He also added another room over the garage for Kenny. Now Kenny had his own room to work on all his electronic projects. With his friend Brian, they created one of the very first computer chess games.

Shortly after the horrible incident at the Munich Olympics in 1972, I took a trip back home to Germany. We did a lot of traveling with my mother, Gerda, Sepp, and Sonja. I didn't know at the time that this was the last time I would see my mother.

When I arrived home again to Fremont, Toby and the kids had acquired a new member of the family. His name was Mu, and he was a Siamese cat. He treated me like I was the newcomer to the house. Mu was such an unusual cat; there are so many stories to tell about him. Before he fell asleep, he would suck on his tail; it was his pacifier. Mu was very smart. When he wanted to come in, he put his paw under the screen door, pulled it and then let go. It sounded like someone was pounding on the door. The trouble was he constantly wanted in and out all day. One day I got real mad and yelled "This is the last time I am going to let you in." When I opened the door, there stood my seventeen-year-old son's friend. He said real quietly, "Hello Mrs. Torngren" I said: "Hi Brian, I thought it was the cat." He probably thought, sure the cat!!

In 1973, Karin joined us here in California. I think she was homesick for all of us. We were so glad to have her with us again. She stayed off and on with us, but most of the time she had her own apartment.

I had joined the Welcome Wagon Club in order to meet friends. One time they organized a gambling bus to Lake Tahoe and Karin and I decided to go together. This was something very new to us and we thought we would have a good time. Well, I am usually very punctual; I always try to be everywhere to the appointed time, most likely even earlier. This time, however I had the date of the trip wrong. I thought we were leaving at 7 Am on Wednesday, when actually it was on Tuesday. I had just gotten up and Karin was still in bed when I received a phone call, "Maya, where are you?" the woman asked, I said "I am at home." "Well, you are supposed to be here on the bus." I was shocked, woke up Karin, and we then dumped everything in a bag, including Karin's hair dryer and took off. Everybody on the bus was kind of grumbling, but I apologized and we were off. When we arrived at the hotel in Lake Tahoe, nobody told us what we were supposed to do. Everybody knew they had to be back in ten minutes to receive their coupons from the Casino..... .everyone except us. Karin said, "Let's just take our time; I take a shower and do my hair, and then we will go gambling." This was OK with me; I was in no hurry. All of a sudden, there was a knock on our door and the woman in charge said, "Why aren't you down at the bus?" I told her that I didn't know we had to be on the bus again. Well, Karin threw some clothes on and with her wet hair; we went down on the bus to get our coupons. This trip had started pretty bad for us, but after a while we had a good time. Most of the women came up to us and told us not to worry any more. However, on the trip home, one woman stood up and tried to really make me feel bad, so I started cry-ing. Then Karin, my usually very quiet daughter, stood up and told her "You'd better leave my mother alone or else you'll have to deal with me." Boy, was I ever proud of her.

Toby always had a funny saying whenever the kids would ask, "What's for dinner?" He would answer "fish heads and rice." One year we went to the Mack Trucks Christmas party. When we came home well after 12 AM we were surprised that all the lights were on and that Susie and Gary were still awake. They were waiting all evening for us to come home. They told us, "We hope you are hungry Dad, because we have a surprise for you." They told Toby to sit down at the table they had set for him. Gary was the waiter with a towel over his arm and he was going to serve him a special treat; a fish head and rice. We all broke up laughing. They told us afterwards that Susie had a friend who came back from fishing with this really big fish and she asked if she could have the head.

Toby was still working on cars. He wanted to fix up cars for each of our kids who now had their driving license. At one time we had a 1963 Studebaker that Toby painted a bright orange. All the kids in the neighborhood called it the "meatloaf."

One day Toby went to his favorite wrecking yard to pick up parts for a car he was working on. When he came home, I found out that he had purchased a wrecked Oldsmobile Vista Cruiser station wagon that they had just towed into the wrecking yard. He couldn't resist it. After fixing the station wagon, he bought an MGB from a worker at Mack. It had been damaged in the right front. Then he found another MGB that had been damaged in the left front. He then bought two more wrecked MGBs and made three good MGBs out of them. This left him with one "MGB skeleton" to get rid off. He did this by burying it in the back yard, covering it with dirt and rocks and then I made a rock garden out of it. I wonder if anybody ever discovered it. While it seemed like our property might have looked bad with all those cars, it really didn't. Toby always managed to have his "projects" out of sight.

In the spring of 1976, my mother died. She fell in her bathtub and I think she must have had a stroke. She died several weeks later. Although I was far away from her in my adult life, I was really very attached to Mama and it hit me pretty hard.

Gerda and Sonja visited us shortly after that. They had planned the trip over here for quite a while. We took them all around to the interesting places in California and of course to San Francisco. We had quite an exciting experience there. We were coming down one of the steep hills and the brakes on our car gave out. Toby stayed calm and coasted down the hill right into a gas station. Like I said before, "Never a dull moment!"

We lived on Bruce Drive in Fremont for almost seven years. During that time, Toby got a new boss. It was the worst boss he had ever had, a very unpleasant human being. (As a matter of fact more than twelve people quit Mack Western because of him.) When Toby finally couldn't take any more of him, he started to look for another job. One of the jobs he applied at was as a designer for a new environmentally friendly car manufacturer in Santa Barbara, my dream city. He also applied for a job at the Freightliner Truck Company in Portland, Oregon. We didn't hear anything from Santa Barbara, but he did get a job offer from Freightliner which he accepted. Soon after that we were moving to Oregon. When the men from the moving company carried our dresser from the master bedroom we saw an unopened letter on the floor. It must have fallen behind the dresser some time ago. It was a job offer from Santa Barbara; nobody remembered seeing that letter before. I was just thinking how our whole life would have been changed, had we found the letter in time. I guess it was destiny.

Only Susie and Gary moved with us to Oregon; Susie happily, Gary reluctantly. He was going to be a senior and didn't appreciate moving at this time. We bought a home in Lake Oswego, just outside of Portland. It was a very contemporary 1920s house. Our kids thought it looked like a post office. Gary had the whole lower floor to himself and grudgingly he even liked Oregon, at least for a while. This was more that can be said of me. I didn't like Oregon at all. It seemed like it was raining all the time and although we had almost two acres of land with fruit trees and a "supposed" view of Mount Hood, most of the time I could only see as far as my clothes line.

We thought Mu would really like all that space, but he was a California cat and he didn't like all that rain either. He just walked once around the house and then wanted to come back in again. But because the front door was very heavy and there was no screen door, there was nowhere Mu could knock on the door—or so we thought. A short time after we let him out the door, there was a knock. We opened the door and there was Mu. We thought somebody must have seen him and knocked for him. The next time we let him out, sure enough, there was a knock, and there he sat. This was too much of a coincidence! So after we let him out the next time, we watched the front door from the side window and saw him leaning with his left paw against the front door and hitting the thumb latch with his right paw. What a clever cat!

I tried to make friends and joined the Welcome Wagon club. One time after the meeting, three women invited me to go with them to a nice restaurant for lunch. I had driven a car that Toby was fixing up for me that wasn't quite finished yet. It must have had at least three different colors. To make sure nobody saw my car, I parked quite far away. The women were very nice to me and I had a good time. When it came time to pay, I noticed that there was no money in my wallet. Sometimes Toby, when he didn't have time to go to the bank, would take money out of my wallet, but he always told me about it, well, this time he didn't. What was I going to do? I had to ask the women, that I barely knew for a loan so I could pay for my lunch. They were very nice about it and told me not to worry. When it was time to go they said, "Maya, where are you parked?" I told them not very far from here. They absolutely wanted to drive me to my car. I of course refused; all I needed was for them to see my car. They might have thought they wouldn't get their money back after they had seen the wreck of a car I was driving.

Lake Oswego was a very nice small town, I would say a little upscale. I remember one time the Welcome Wagon had a party with the husbands invited and the men were saying to Toby, not "Did you go to college?" but rather, "Which college did you graduate from?"

Gary had just received his driver's license and had bought himself a car. Once when he was on vacation, I rode with him from Oregon to California. Since it was his car and he was driving, he made the rules. They were: no stopping for lunch or dinner, we could only make rest stops. We made it almost all the way to Fremont, when I felt really sick to my stomach and I told him if he didn't stop I wouldn't be responsible for what would happen to his car. That of course did the trick.

On one of the times that I was visiting Karin and Kenny in San Jose, Kenny asked me if I wanted to go for a ride in his Fiat X 19, a neat little sports car. It sounded like fun, and off we went. I never knew before that San Jose's hills are pretty good sized mountains. We drove up to Mount Umunum, the farther up we got, the narrower the road was. It was deja vu for me. It felt just like in the Canary Islands when there was nothing on either side of the narrow mountain road, only this time it was in sports car.

Toby and I also drove back to San Jose for Kenny's graduation from San Jose State University. He was the first in the family to get a degree; his was in Electrical Engineering. Karin and Gary eventually got Bachelor degrees, and Susie, a Master's in Speech Therapy.

Susie met her husband to-be at the bank where she worked. She went to college in Corvallis, Oregon, and on Christmas Eve 1978 Susie and Al got married and soon after moved to Anchorage, Alaska.

Living in Oregon with all that rain and so little light, I was depressed for the first time in my life.

Toby finally said that we would move back to California again. He got his old job back (his old boss was gone), but he had to start work right away. So Gary and I were left in Oregon until we sold the house. One time we had a terrible ice storm. I had never seen anything like that. The biggest trees were bent over the roads and many of them broke like match sticks. We were without heat and electricity for almost a week and, to top it all off, the water pipes froze. Gary was the man of the house and he really came through for me.

We finally sold the house and Toby bought a house in Hayward, California for us, sight unseen by me. I did have an idea what the house might look like since I went down once to California to go house hunting, but we didn't find anything at that time.

We moved into our almost new home in the Hayward hills (with a swimming pool). Gary was very impressed and we all enjoyed the pool. Toby and I didn't have any work with the pool; Gary maintained it. We thought we were set for life, but it wasn't meant to be.

Mack Trucks closed down operations on the West Coast in 1981, and it would have meant moving to Allentown, Pennsylvania. We just didn't want to do that, so Toby was once again without a job. Since he was one of the most reliable employees, he was the last to leave. By that time, there were no more jobs available in the area. We had to sell our big house in Hayward and buy something cheaper, very much cheaper. It turned out to be a little old fixer-upper house in Atascadero. It was in such bad shape that when Karin said goodbye to us, after helping us move in, she started to cry. She felt so bad to leave us there, all alone in that decrepit house. But we were optimistic. We had big plans of making a living out of remodeling houses. But times were bad, interest rates were 17%, and things just didn't work out. Since we made money on the previous house, we lived quite comfortably there for three years.

I really liked the Central Coast. Atascadero was a very nice small town with beautiful scenery all around. We were only 1/2 hour away from Morro Bay. When the weather was hot in Atascadero, we just drove over to the coast and it was sometimes thirty degrees cooler there. We soon learned that we had to wear jackets, and certainly not shorts, because it could be quite cold, especially when you just came from 90 to 100 degree weather.

One year, while Toby's sister Dorrit was visiting us, we had quite a large earthquake. It destroyed the little town of Coalinga, not too far away from where we were living. This was Dorrit's first experience in an earthquake. She lived all her life in Michigan where there are no earthquakes. The two of us were inside when it happened. It was a very heavy jolt and the first thing we did was to hold on to all my treasures (Hummel figurines etc.) They all rattled on the shelves, but didn't break. Toby was outside next to his truck and he watched the truck bounce up and down. Quite an experience!!!

I have always been an avid reader and I don't usually go for recommended books. However, Susie introduced me to John Steinbeck and he turned out to be my favorite author. (Maybe I should listen more often.) I read almost all of his books. While living in Atascadero, I sometimes took the bus from Paso Robles up to San Jose to visit our kids. There usually were some buses that stopped in only a few towns like King City and Salinas. There was also one bus that stopped just about everywhere, as I was to find out. I was just settling down with my book, John Steinbeck's, "The Wayward Bus" when I noticed that the bus left Highway 101 and drove on very small roads. The most interesting part was that as I was reading this story I saw it come alive for me. I noticed that many of the places that I saw from the bus were mentioned in the book. The bus stopped whenever someone wanted to get on or off. Although it took a long time to get to San Jose, this was the greatest bus ride ever for me.

In January 1982, Karin and Dave got married in San Jose, and I was to help with the preparation for the wedding. I drove up on a Monday and the next day we had one of the worst storms I had ever experienced in California. Part of Highway 1 fell into the Pacific, and the highway was closed from Monterey on. It didn't reopen until two years later. Highway 101 was also closed because of flooding, and we were worried that Toby wouldn't make it to San Jose for the wedding. Luckily, the highway opened again on Friday. We almost didn't have a wedding cake since the lady who was going to bake it lost her house in a landslide in the Santa Cruz Mountains. But in spite of all that, it was a very nice wedding.

When Dave joined our family, he brought something very special to us. There always was affection in our family, but since both of us came from a northern European family background, there wasn't much OPEN affection. Thanks to Dave, now when we all get together, there is a lot of hugging going on, where there wasn't much before and it really feels good.

During this time, Susie was working at Wien Airlines in Alaska. We had great flying privileges and took several trips to Alaska and Europe. Once we were in Anchorage, we could just go to the airport and for 10 dollars we could fly to any-where in Alaska. We really took advantage of this. One time we flew to Barrow, the farthest northern town in Alaska (you could see the polar ice cap from the shore). There was absolutely nothing growing there and many of the homes were made out of shipping containers. Everybody had a snowmobile and an ATV, (all-terrain vehicle) and when the vehicles broke down; they just parked them and bought another one. All their lives, they had been throwing out things in the winter and in the spring there wouldn't be anything left to see, but a snowmobile cannot be eaten, nor would it rot. This made the area look like a junk yard.

Another time we flew to Nome and then took a bush plane over to St. Lawrence Island, where you could see Siberia when the weather was nice. On the way over, we had one fellow passenger, a young Eskimo girl who was coming home from college. The "airport terminal" on the island was a very small shed with a flag on it. It seemed like the whole village had turned out for her arrival. They all came to greet her on their all-terrain vehicles (like a four-wheel motorcycle). We found out later that the girl was from a very prominent family on the island.

We walked around the island while waiting for supplies to be unloaded from the plane. It was wild and rugged and very interesting. When it was time to go back, we were the only passengers and the pilot asked Toby if he wanted to sit up front with him. Of course, he did. Since the flight over was a little hectic, I just sat in the back of the plane and was reading a book to get my mind off this trip. After we landed, Toby asked me how the flight was. I told him it was better than the trip over to the island. That's when he told me that the pilot had asked him if he wanted to fly back while he did his paper work; naturally he did. Toby had already taken some flying lessons in Hayward in a small plane, but this one was a twin engine plane and more fun for him.

We also took a plane to Juno, which is the capitol of Alaska and can only be reached by ship or plane. After landing in Juno, we rented a car and took in all the sights, including Mendenhall Glacier, which was very interesting.

On my birthday in 1983, our Mu died. Gary and Kenny were visiting us at that time. We buried him on our hill and I planted California poppies over his grave.

While Susie was working for the airlines, she gave both Toby and I a very special present. For her dad it was a trip to Australia and for me a trip to Germany at Christmas time. I hadn't spent Christmas in Germany since I left in 1952, and this was 1983. Christmas is always such a special time in Germany. Susie and I arrived in Augsburg a week before Christmas and could participate in all the special things that were going on around this time of year, like the "Christkindle's Markt" (Christ Child market) in front of the Rathaus Platz (City Hall Square) and of course we admired all the decorations in and outside the big department stores.

We celebrated Christmas Eve at Gerda and Sepp's apartment. It is the custom to make many different kinds of fancy cookies and Gerda really outdid herself;

she must have made at least twelve different kinds. The Christmas tree was still lit with candles, just like it was when I was growing up. At midnight, we strolled through town, arm in arm, my sister Gerda, my niece Sonja, my daughter Susie, and I with the snow crunching under our feet. The church bells were ringing all over town, ringing in the Christmas night. The Christmas Mass had already started by the time we arrived at the Dom, Augsburg's largest cathedral (dated back to 823 AD.) This brought back some good memories for me, (even in wartime, there were still some of those). Susie and I truly had a wonderful time.

My sister lives on the first floor of a twenty-one-story apartment building. Her daughter Sonja had an apartment on the fifteenth floor. On New Years Eve, we all took the elevator up to her apartment to bring in the New Year. This turned out to be quite an experience. At midnight we could see and hear the fire-works all over Augsburg. It sounded like the city was under artillery attack. This was one New Years Eve I will never forget.

By 1984, we could see that we had to move back to the Bay Area again. We bought a house in Fremont with Kenny as a co-owner. Once again it was a fixer-upper and Toby had to put a lot of his labor into it. He now was working for FMC in San Jose. He went from designing cars (in Michigan) to trucks (Hayward, Ca. and Portland, Or.) to fighting vehicles at FMC, quite a change.

Although we had lived in Fremont before, I had been away too long to know very many people any more. So I joined the New in Town Club. They had all kinds of planned activities and since I always had liked to do needlework of any kind I asked if there was a group like that available. They told me no, but they had a quilting group. They said bring whatever you are working on and join us. After seeing all the beautiful quilts everybody was making, I decided to try quilting myself. This was the beginning of a wonderful creative outlet for me. Quilting became a great hobby for me from then on.

Early one morning, while we were still asleep, somebody pounded on our front door to let us know that the neighbor's house was on fire. Our bedroom was only a few feet away from the burning home and we could hear the fire roaring away. The fire department arrived quickly and soon had the fire out. The neighbor's house was badly damaged.

Something wonderful happened on April 17, 1985, our very first grandchild, Ingrid Marie Waisanen, was born. We were such proud grandparents. We had waited such a long time for a grandchild. Karin and I flew up to Anchorage to see the new baby.

In October 1985, Gary and Lisa were married. We couldn't have hoped for a better daughter-in-law. They had an authentic Philippine wedding with all of their good food (this was the first time we had had lumpias). There were also Hawaiian hula dancers and to our surprise Gary joined in the dancing. We had never seen a bride and groom dance, where everybody pinned money on to the bride and groom's clothing while dancing with them. We all had a great time.

The same year, Toby and I took a trip to Europe, visiting relatives in Denmark and Germany. We took lots of trips with my sister Gerda and her husband Sepp and also my cousin Helmut, his wife Hanna and their daughter Claudia. One time we met them at Lake Garda, Italy, in an outdoor restaurant at a specific time, the four of us and the three of them coming from a different direction and the timing was right, which surprised us all. We all stayed together at a hotel and from there took a side trip to Venice. Hanna was our guide. She was so well informed and we learned things we never would have known on our own. No matter where we went, Hanna could tell us the history of the place. I will never forget the good times we had together.

Gerda, Sepp, Toby, and I also took a bus trip to Yugoslavia to see the Plitvice lakes and falls. The scenery was spectacular but the people were all dressed in dark clothes and were not a happy lot.

On July 17, 1986, we were blessed with another granddaughter named Laura Ann. I was up in Anchorage taking care of Ingrid while Susie was in the hospital. We were only very sad that they were so far away from us. We really missed seeing the girls grow up.

By 1989, the real estate market was going wild and since Toby was going to retire in 1992, we thought we would buy an "investment house." It was an attached house in the Villages in San Jose, a retirement community. We even had to be in a lottery just to be able to get a new house there. We sold our house in Fremont in less than a week and moved to San Jose. It was a very nice place to live, very quiet and we liked it a lot.

While we were there, the Loma Prieta earthquake hit the Bay Area in December 1989. It was the worst earthquake we had ever experienced. We weren't far from the epicenter. There was a lot of damage in San Francisco, Oakland, and Santa Cruz.

On Thanksgiving in 1990, it happened that everybody in the family had to be somewhere else. So Toby and I had to spend the holiday by ourselves. We thought a turkey would be too big for just the two of us, so we decided to have the ducks that we had in the freezer. They had been given to Toby by a co-worker who was a hunter. Since it was a beautiful, sunny fall day, we decided to cook the ducks outside on the barbeque. Toby made a great fire; we put on the ducks, and went inside. After a little while, we went out to check on the ducks and found a roaring fire, with flames coming up out of the barbeque and smoke as high as the house, drifting over to the neighbor's lot. Toby ran and got the garden hose and shortly the fire was under control. What was left were two charred carcasses. There was no duck dinner that day; our Thanksgiving feast ended up being hot dogs. "Flaming duck a'la orange" was not on the menu that day.

As the homeowner's fees were very high (and Toby didn't really want to stay in the Bay Area), we realized that it was a very expensive area to live in after Toby retired. So we decided to sell and look for another house outside of the Bay Area.

Once, when Toby was visiting Denmark with his sister Dorrit, I invited my two best quilting friends Nancy and Ruth to stay with me for a couple of days. One afternoon, we had a lot of fun at the Arts and Crafts Fair in San Juan Bautista. On the way back we had to stop for gas in Gilroy. I had never filled the gas tank by myself. Toby always did this for me. Well, my friends weren't much help either, but we finally got it done. In the evening, we were sitting around the living room when a big storm came and all the lights went out. We were sitting in the dark, drinking a few drinks and giggling together. All of a sudden it sounded like the front door was rattling, it probably was just the wind, but it scared the living daylights out of us. We thought somebody was trying to get in.

At our next Guild meeting we read in the newsletter the following:

"JOKE OF THE MONTH"

How many quilters does it take to fill a gas tank at a self-service gas station? ... Only three if they are resourceful! One to determine which side of the car the gas tank is on, one to read the owners' manual to find out how to release the gas cap, and one to figure out how the gas pump works! This was reported after a recent outing in Gilroy. Could it be it had something to do with the air in Gilroy?

In September 1991, we bought a home in a retirement community in Vacaville. Once again, we bought an old house that needed everything fixed up. Every Friday we drove up to Vacaville to work on the house and then came back early Monday morning when Toby had to go back to work.

When Toby was ready to retire in February 1992, we were done with the house in Vacaville and moved up there. We couldn't sell our house in San Jose at that time because the real estate market went way down, so we rented it out. The house in Vacaville was located in Leisure Town, a retirement community. All of the homes there backed up to a green strip. It was home to a lot of rabbits and quail. They visited us often in our yard, but they were never a nuisance. We enjoyed watching the wildlife, especially the quail. One time we found twenty quail eggs in our garden and shortly afterwards we watched sixteen live baby quail coming out of their shells. They started running right away with Mama Quail and Papa Quail leading the way.

I had started a garden where there was none before. It was beautiful, especially in the spring time. We also had a fig tree with all the figs we could eat. We planted two cherry trees and in just two years we had lots and lots of black cherries. We did have to fight the birds to get our share, somehow they wanted them all.

Just outside the sliding glass door there was an unsightly pyracanta bush that I wanted to cut down, but Toby wanted to keep it. One day he told me to come outside to look at something. He had trimmed the Pyracanta bush into the shape of a big heart for me. Of course I agreed to keep the bush; how could I not!! He is such a romantic!!

At this time, I joined two quilting groups and met many local quilters who became good friends. We always had a lot of fun together. I made many small quilts, but my two favorites are "Homes I lived in" showing all the homes I lived in during my life in America and "The trip of a Lifetime" depicting all the places we had been to on our trip. Toby had challenged me to do those two quilts and I received much praise and ribbons for them, but most importantly, I love those two quilts.

One afternoon in 1993, we were walking around in the little town of Winters, not far from Vacaville, when we heard some band music and saw that there was a concert band playing in the park. We stayed and listened and afterwards the conductor invited everybody who ever played an instrument to join the Yolo County Concert Band. I urged Toby to go up there and talk to the man, which he did. Toby hadn't played an instrument for over forty years. He attended the next rehearsal and was now a member of the band, playing either the trumpet or the horn. Toby now had his very own hobby that he enjoyed as much as I do quilting. Soon after, one of the band members started a swing band and Toby played the trumpet there as well. They played for dances for seniors and other occasions. We, the wives of the band members, danced together to the music and it was always great fun for me. It reminded me of my youth when the swing bands were playing in Germany and quite often I danced with my girlfriend Anni. Toby soon was playing full time in the "Yolo County Concert Band," the "It's About Time" Swing Band, and part time in the "Sonoma Hometown Band," the Eldorado Brass Band, and other small groups.

Gary and Lisa moved to an older home in Sonoma with beautiful views all around. It needed a lot of work and Toby was glad to help them. On November

7, 1995, Michael Christopher Torngren was born to his very happy parents, Gary and Lisa. We were so excited that now we also had a grandson. He was such a good little boy and we all love him so much. When he was about two years old we could see that he had a big problem, he couldn't communicate verbally. He was wrongly diagnosed and from then on, Gary and Lisa went through a very rough time. He had delayed speech, but was very intelligent in every other way.

In the spring of 1996, Gerda, Sepp and Sonja visited us from Germany. They flew to Texas to see Susie and her family. Toby and I drove to Austin to meet them. While we were there, Susie received her degree in speech therapy from the University of Texas in Austin. We all went to the outdoor graduation festivities at the University. After a few days of touring Texas, we were on our way back to California. We drove through New Mexico, Arizona, Utah, and Nevada. We saw the Grand Canyon, Bryce Canyon, and Zion National Park. I have traveled a lot around the world, but never have I been so impressed as I was at seeing the Grand Canyon for the first time. It is awe inspiring and for a few moments it leaves you speechless. I think Bryce Canyon, Zion National Park, and the Painted Dessert are also very beautiful. It was a great trip that still lingers in my memory. Needless to say, my German relatives were also very impressed.

Maya the unhappy truck driver

Our cat "Mu"

Fish head and rice

Our home in Fremont, to the left of our neighbor's burning house. "Too close for comfort".

Our granddaughters, Laura and Ingrid

Our grandson, Michael

THE TWILIGHT YEARS

On August 8th, 2000, I came home from my quilt meeting and found Toby in very bad shape. He had had a small stroke. I called 911 and he was taken to the hospital. This was on Thursday, but they released him the next day. On Saturday morning, Toby insisted on playing with the Concert Band that afternoon in Vacaville. I tried everything I could think of to talk him out of it but to no avail. The reason he was so persistent was that he wanted to be part of the band playing the music from the musical "I do I do" for me (as he was now unsure of his health). This musical deals with the marriage of a couple from the night before their wedding until the day they leave their home of over fifty years. The one number that meant the most to him was, "My Cup Runneth Over With Love."[1]

The lyrics are as follows:

Sometimes in the morning when shadows are deep
I lie here beside you just watching you sleep
and sometimes I whisper what I'm thinking of
My cup runneth over with love

Sometimes in the evening when you do not see
I study the small things you do constantly
I memorize moments that I'm fondest of
My cup runneth over with love

In only a moment we both will be old
We won't even notice the world turning cold
and so in this moment with sunlight above
My cup runneth over with love

We have been so fortunate to have a love like ours for so many years.

In October 2000, Gary, Lisa and Michael moved to a new home in Oakdale and by December we bought a house in the same subdivision. We wanted to be close to be of help to them in any way we could.

While our home was being built in Oakdale, we drove to Austin, Texas to stay with Susie and her family. It was so nice to be close to our granddaughters. We have been apart for such a long time and had to make up for lost time. We were able to celebrate Easter and also Ingrid's sixteenth birthday together.

After five weeks, we drove back to California and rented an apartment in Modesto, since it was going to take longer for us to move into our new house than expected.

When we lived in Atascadero, a woman friend said to me once, "Maya you have lived a charmed life; nothing has ever gone terribly wrong for you," and I had to agree THEN.

One always dreads the phone call one receives in the middle of the night, but this worst of all phone calls came on a beautiful June afternoon, when we heard that Ingrid had been very seriously injured in a Jet Ski accident. Karin flew to Austin and stayed with her sister and Ingrid at the hospital, hoping against hope until the end. Ingrid died on June 12, 2001. This was the worst moment of my life; I guess my "charmed" life was over. Ingrid had willed to have her organs donated in case of her death. Some part of Ingrid is living in many people, but most importantly she is living in our hearts.

We moved into our new home in July 2001. I have again made many good friends here in Oakdale, all in my quilt group. It was quite a challenge to plant the big hill behind our house, but it is slowly looking very good.

On March 8th, 2002 we celebrated our 50th wedding anniversary. Since my sister Gerda and my niece Sonja were coming from Germany in May, we had the actual party at that time. We all got together (only Susie and her family were missing) at a restaurant in Knight's Ferry, located directly by the river. Gerda was the only one who actually was present at our wedding fifty years ago. It was a real nice party.

In October 2003, Toby had a routine colonoscopy that detected a cancerous polyp, and had an operation to remove it on December 8th. He was released from the hospital after ten days, only to have to go back again. I was called by his doctor and was told that unfortunately, he had to have another operation, two more resections of his small intestines. I was all alone at home and so was Gary; he had a very bad cold and couldn't come over to comfort me or me him. It was a very long wait until we finally found out that the operation was successful. However, they kept Toby in the hospital for one whole month after that. Karin and Susie went with me to the hospital every day, and Gary came very often after work. I was so grateful for all their help. We were hoping for Toby to be home for Christmas, but that wasn't meant to be. Karin and I spent Christmas Eve, first at the hospital, and then with Lisa, Gary and Michael. At the hospital, they gave Toby so many powerful drugs that he often was completely out of it. Karin talked it over with his doctor and it was decided not to give him any more of those drugs that he was having a very bad reaction to.

After Toby was home again and the worst was over, he got a crazy look on his face, looked me right in the eyes and told me, "But I am doing much better now" (this came from a TV show "Night Court" where the judge's father, was telling his son about his stay in a mental institution and had been released, and was explaining, "But I am doing much better now") Toby is a great joker and says this once in a while. We always know when he is joking again, that things are looking up.

In the meantime Michael went from Kindergarten to first grade and now is going into third grade. He is doing very well in school. The first few years he had his own aid and a dynamo to make up for his lack of speech. The Oakdale school district has been very good to him, giving him access to several speech therapy classes each week. Just a few months ago, Michael finally started to speak. We are so thrilled for every word we hear him say. He finally can tell us how he feels. Just recently, we had a Fathers' day party at our house and he told us he was bored. He also told us, "I love you Oma, and I love you Grandpa" and Toby really liked it when he said, "Grandpa you are funny."

Karin and Dave bought a nice eighty-year old bungalow in Willow Glen in San Jose with a big swimming pool. Michael just loves the water and said the other day to his uncle Dave, "Do you have any swimming pool accessories?" It was one of his very first sentences. We were just so amazed. Everybody takes speech for granted, but to hear Michael speak now is like a gift, although a very hard one earned by him and his parents.

I am sad to say that Susie and Al got divorced. Things never were the same after Ingrid's death. However, Susie and Laura moved back to California, near Karin's home. It is so great to have the whole family together again.

February 26th, 2004, I celebrated my 75th birthday. I have come a long way since my 15th birthday in the basement of my home when my hometown went up in flames and smoke. I have a husband that I love so very much and that loves me, and four great children and two wonderful grandchildren. Even after some heart-aches, I still feel blessed.

From top left: Gary, Lisa, Sonja, Dave, Karin. Bottom from left: Gerda, Maya, Toby, Michael and Ken at our 50th wedding anniversary

Maya in front of the "Heart" Pyracanta bush

"Homes I've lived in" quilt

"The trip of a lifetime" quilt

978-0-595-44345-1
0-595-44345-1